57046
50

The

The Fall ot New France in 1760

Michael Phifer

Michael Phifer

The Last Campaign: The Fall of New France in 1760

(Front cover illustration: A South View of Oswego ca. 1760 Library and Archives Canada .)

Copyright © 2013 Michael Phifer
All rights reserved. No part of this publication may be
reproduced in any form or by any means without
permission from the author.

ISBN:9781482329445

Other Books by Author:

Wolves From Niagara: Butler's Ranger 1777-1784

Lifeline: The War of 1812 Along the Upper St. Lawrence River

Gunsmoke and Lead: Canadian Born Lawmen and Outlaws in the American Old West

Gunfire Along the River: A Concise History of the Battle of Crysler's Farm, November 11, 1813

Edited by:
A Redcoat and Greencoat at War: The Narratives of Shadrach Byfield of the 41st Regiment and Thaddeus Lewis of the Glengarry Light Infantry

To some of my ancestors who endured the war on the New York frontier.

THE LAST CAMPAIGN: THE FALL OF NEW FRANCE IN 1760

CONTENTS

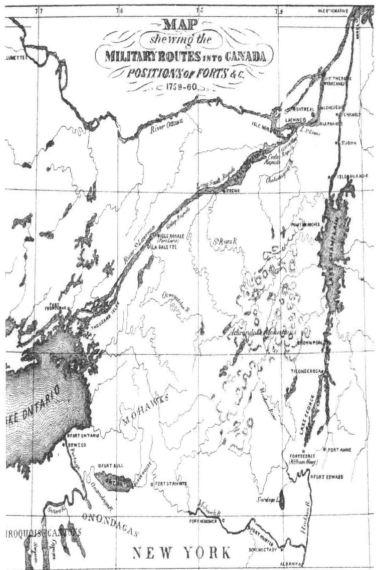

From *The History of Canada Under French Regime 1535-1763.*

Introduction

I t was the war that forever changed the course of history in North America. Territorial expansion between France and England in the Ohio Valley led to a violent confrontation in the backwoods of Pennsylvania in the late spring and summer of 1754 that would escalate into a worldwide war. England and France had been at war with each other three times between 1689 and 1748. These limited bloody wars were fought over the balance of power in Europe and were carried over to the new world where they were known as King William's War, Queen Anne's War and King George's War. This new bigger war (called by historians the Seven Years' War or the French and Indian War in the U.S.) that started on the American frontier would be about more than just the balance of power. The conquest of a vast amount of territory was at stake in this conflict. Although it would not be until 1756 that war was officially declared between France and England and campaigns would eventually be conducted in

Europe, the Caribbean, India and Africa, serious fighting by that time was already raging in North America.

At first glance it would seem the odds favored the English colonies in a war with New France. The population of the 14 British colonies stretching from Nova Scotia to Georgia numbered about 1,500,000, while the population of New France numbered about 70,000. There were, however, more factors than numbers. The British colonies did not present a united front often being in dispute with one another, while New France was centralized under one governor with a well honed militia adroit in wilderness warfare. Through New France's long history in the fur trade, the French could count on many Indian allies (at least at the start of the war).

The French were quickly to show that numbers did not mean everything as they were to hand the Anglo-American forces a series of major defeats near the Forks of the Ohio, Oswego and Fort William Henry in the first few years of the war which shocked the British colonies. Adding to the misery were French and Indian war parties sweeping down on the frontier from the Mohawk Valley to Virginia leaving burnout cabins and bodies in their wake.

Not all was doom and gloom as the American provincials under William Johnson achieved a victory a Lake George in 1755. That same year the British achieved a darker victory in the east coast of Canada with the expulsion of the Acadians. It would not be until 1758 when the tide would begin to turn in the war for the British with the fall of Fort Duquesne, Louisbourg and the destruction of Fort Frontenac. The British did not have things all their own way as they were repulsed at Ticonderoga. The following year would see a string of victories at Niagara, Ticonderoga and Quebec that would set the stage for the last campaign of 1760. This is a concise military account of that campaign.

To avoid confusion a note should be made here on a few things. I have used the name of Canada and New France interchangeably in this work. The inhabitants of Canada I have called Canadian which at the time of course were all French. The location of La Galette also might cause some confusion. Originally La Galette was a small trading fort established possibly as early as 1682 on the north shore of the St. Lawrence near modern Johnstown, Ontario where it was abandoned and re-occupied a few times. Across the river on the south side in modern Ogdensburg, New York was Fort La Presentation built in 1749. Because of the close proximity, La Presentation was often referred to by the English as La Galette. In this work I have used La Galette interchangeably with La Presentation.

Chapter 1
Victory Incomplete: 1759

Sir William Johnson had good reason to be pleased. The army he commanded had dealt the French a mighty blow. On July 25, 1759, the vital link to New France's western post on the Great Lakes and the Ohio River had been cut. The Union flag now fluttered over Fort Niagara.

The campaign to take Niagara had started two months earlier when Brigadier-General John Prideaux had been ordered by Major-General Jeffery Amherst, the commander-in-chief of British forces in North America, to advance up the Mohawk Valley with a force of 5,000 regulars and provincials with the intentions of taking Fort Niagara. After leaving a strong garrison at Fort Stanwix in the western end of the valley, Prideaux pushed onto Oswego. There he found Sir William Johnson, waiting for him with a 1,000 Iroquois warriors.

Sir William Johnson (Library of Congress).

Called "Warraghiyagey" which roughly means "a man who undertakes great things", William Johnson had great influence among the Six Nations, especially the Mohawks who he had been neighbours with since 1738 when he came from Ireland to the Mohawk Valley of New York to oversee his uncle's, Vice-Admiral Sir Peter Warren, estate. Through land acquisitions; his connection with the Iroquois, the fur trade and other ventures, Johnson had become quite successful in the new world. His connection with the Iroquois led to his being appointed to the position of Northern Superintendent of Indian Affairs in 1755, the same year he received a baronetcy for his victory over the French at Lake George.

Leaving 1,000 men to rebuilt Fort Ontario at Oswego under the command of Colonel Frederick Haldimand[1] of the Royal American Regiment, Prideaux with the rest of his force rowed along the southern shore of Lake Ontario towards Fort Niagara. On July 6, the army arrived before Niagara and the siege began. Part way into the siege Johnson suddenly found himself in command when Prideaux accidently had the back of his head blown off by a mortar. As the siege lines crept closer to Fort Niagara, word soon arrived in the British and American camp that a French relief force was on its way. The relief force was stopped cold with most of the French and Canadian troops

---

[1] Born in Switzerland in 1718, Fredrick Haldimand was a veteran officer of the Prussian army, as well as the Swiss Guards of the Dutch army. In 1756 he joined the British army serving in the newly raised Royal Americans (62nd shortly changed to the 60th). While rebuilding Fort Oswego, Haldimand repulsed a French attack against his camp while Niagara was under siege.

Brigadier-General Gage (Library and Archives Canada).

being killed, wounded or captured. Captain Pierre Pouchot, the commandant of Fort Niagara, upon hearing of the defeat had no choice but to surrender the fort. On August 5, Johnson left Niagara in the command of a regular officer and set out for Oswego arriving two days later to find work still progressing on Fort Ontario. Johnson would not be in charge there long as on August 16 Brigadier-General Thomas Gage[2] arrived with orders from Amherst to take command.

Upon taking command, Gage's orders from Amherst were clear. If Niagara was already in British hands, then Gage was to build a fleet and move down the St. Lawrence River and take the weak fort at La Galette.[3] From there he was to push on for Montreal. The British campaign to drive into Canada to aid Major-General James Wolfe besieging

---

[2] Born in Ireland in 1719, Gage saw service in the War of Austrian Succession and at Culloden during the Jacobite Rebellion. In 1755 he arrived in North America where he survived Braddock's bloody defeat near the Forks of the Ohio River. In late 1757 he proposed forming a regular light infantry unit to be trained in regular and irregular combat. The plan was accepted and the unit became the 80th.

[3] Technically La Presentation, but popularly known as La Galette by the British. See introduction.

Quebec had stalled in the late summer of 1759 and Amherst wanted Gage to get things moving again. He was to be disappointed.

At the beginning of the year Amherst's orders from William Pitt, Britain's war leader, had been clear. The attack against Canada was to come from two directions; recommendations Amherst had made himself. While Wolfe was to move against Quebec, Amherst was to invade Canada from the south either by way of Crown Point or La Galette. If it was practical he was to attack Montreal or Quebec or both. Amherst other orders were to re-establish a post at Oswego along Lake Ontario and capture Fort Niagara.

While these last orders were being carried out, Amherst led his force of 11,000 regulars and provincials by water north towards Ticonderoga.[4] Four days after Amherst's army landed and had their guns emplaced ready for a siege, the French spiked their guns and blew up the fort. They retreated down Lake Champlain to Crown Point[5] to join the 3,000 troops under Brigadier-General Francois-Charles de Bourlamaque.[6] The French demolished the fort there and continued their retreat north. They took up a position at Isle-aux-Noix on the Richelieu River where a fort had been under construction since May to protect the

---

[4] Called Fort Carillon by the French.

[5] Called Fort St. Frederic by the French.

[6] Bourlamaque who was possibly of Italian decent, was born in Paris in 1716. He joined the French army in 1739 as a volunteer and rose through the ranks seeing combat in the War of the Austrian Succession. He was sent to New France in 1756 and would see action at Oswego, Fort William Henry and Ticonderoga.

southern approach to Montreal.

On August 4, Amherst arrived at the strewn rubble of Crown Point. Here he began work on an elaborate fort which was to secure all the country south of it. This delayed his advance as did the beginning of building a brigantine, floating battery and sloop to allow Captain Joshua Loring[7] of the Royal Navy to face the French four vessels at the foot of Lake Champlain.

Amherst was not the only one delaying his advance into New France. Despite the commander-in-chief's order to move down the St. Lawrence River, Gage tarried at Oswego. When Gage took over command from Johnson he showed him his orders from Amherst to take La Galette and establish a post there. Gage had other ideas though. He believed there was not enough time to establish and supply a post at La Galette. As it was they had only about three weeks worth of provisions for the troops at Oswego, although cattle were on their way.

If Gage was reluctant to attack La Galette, Johnson was not. Johnson asked Colonel Haldimand directly if Gage had said anything to him about moving on La Galette. Haldimand replied that he had seen Amherst's orders, but Gage had said nothing about taking La Galette. Johnson thought it was practical to destroy the place and said as much, but added it would be impossible to construct a

---

[7] Joshua Loring was born in Roxbury (near Boston) in 1716 and worked as an apprentice tanner. In 1744, he became a privateer commanding a brigantine. He was captured by the French and spent a few months as a prisoner in Louisbourg. In 1745, Loring was commissioned a lieutenant in the Royal Navy. Eleven years later he was promoted to commander.

strong fort this late in the season. Like Gage, Johnson thought provisioning a post on the Upper St. Lawrence River would prove difficult. Haldimand agreed.

Johnson was relentless on the idea of destroying La Galette. Gage, however, was more reluctant not wanting to tarnish his honour by "attempting impossibilities" explaining to Johnson the state of his artillery, ammunition and provisions. Although Johnson understood the general's concern, he still stated his case of destroying La Galette, but not attempting to establish a post there. Gage seemed lacklustre about the idea.

Two days later on the 20th, Johnson met again with Gage on the subject this time showing the general a rough draft of the St. Lawrence River from Fort Frontenac to an island just below La Galette drawn by an Onondaga Indian named Red Head.[8] After dining together, Gage and Johnson took a walk to discuss more about taking the French post to which the general finally agreed to once the artillery and vessels were made ready. No move was made though. Johnson and his Indian Department officers, meanwhile, busied themselves recruiting warriors to accompany Gage's expedition.

On a rainy August 31, Johnson learned a wealth of information about the enemy from a German born deserter named Henry Young, who had been serving with the French. Young had seen a fair amount of service on the Upper St. Lawrence being at La Galette and Oswegatchie,

---

[8] Ononwarogo was an Onondaga warrior known to the British as Red Head or Young Red Head. The "young" was gradually dropped after his father, who was also called Red Head (Kak8enthion) by the British, died in 1756.

an Indian village near the fort.

The fort at La Galette, according to Young, was square and consisted of four blockhouses and a stockade. The French had intended to do some additional work around the fort last spring but ran out of time. The fort had a couple of weakness most notably the commanding rising ground about 400 paces from it. There were also no cannons or mortars at the fort. A thousand barrels of flour and pork were taken from the fort and moved to the nearby Isle Royale, also known as Orakointon,[9] when word came that the British were planning on coming down river. The provisions were only kept on the island for about three weeks before they were moved by two French vessels a little further upriver to Pointe-au- Baril.[10]

From Young is was also learned that a sizeable workforce had been on Isle Royale cutting down trees, digging a trench and making breastworks of logs filled with earth twelve feet broad. Twelve 12-pounders were mounted in the breastworks with the intention of firing on any enemy bateaux moving down river. Stones from Oswegatchie had been moved to the island to built ovens, powder magazines and a dwelling house.

Gage still made no signs of moving on La Galette. On September 1, Johnson fitted out a party of Senecas and Oneidas to obtain prisoners from the French post if possible and gain all the intelligence they could on troop strength and the location of the vessels. The scouting party

---

[9] Modern Chimney Island.
[10] Modern Maitland, Ontario.

also took with them black and white wampum to give to the Oswegatchies as a warning to get out of the British's way and "quit the French interest."[11]

That same day the Onondagas requested that Johnson would stop another party heading to Oswegatchie to be replaced by one of their own so they could warn the Oswegatchies to leave their village. Johnson refused. The fact that the Onondagas would want to warn the Oswegatchies of any coming trouble is not surprising. The Oswegatchies were actually Onondagas who had converted to Catholicism and had moved to their new home along the upper St. Lawrence River ten years earlier.

On the afternoon of September 6, Johnson again talked with Gage on attacking La Galette. Gage spoke freely telling the Indian Superintendent that Amherst had missed his opportunity in helping Wolfe at Quebec by not pushing north into Canada, which in Gage's opinion was too late in the season. An expedition against La Galette now would do little service. In fact, Gage thought his little army had done more than Amherst's army and they would do well if they could finish Fort Ontario and keep it and Fort Niagara supplied. Gage would not long after write to Amherst telling his superior he was not going to make any venture against La Galette or Montreal this season. Amherst would not be pleased.

Even as any move against La Galette seemed unlikely, Gage met with some of his officers at noon on the 7th

---

[11] James Sullivan (editor), *The Papers of Sir William Johnson Vol. 13*, (Albany: University of New York, 1962). p. 133.

asking if anyone of them knew a thing or two about sea-faring operations. He was interested in capturing the two French vessels operating on the Upper St. Lawrence River and Lake Ontario. After the consultation it was decided Captain Parker would make an attempt against the enemy vessels with a cutting-out party of volunteers.

A strong wind and rain kept the cutting-out party from slipping out of Oswego the following morning. Finally on the morning of the 8th, the party rowed out in search of the French vessels. Parker's command consisted of 250 men, along with a handful of Mohawks.

In the end Parker and his men failed to take the enemy vessels, but were successful in capturing four French sailors who had gone ashore to hunt on the 11th. These prisoners revealed Brigadier-General Francois-Gaston, Duc de Levis had 2,000 men entrenching on Isle Royale. There was some truth to their information.

Upon hearing of the fall of Fort Niagara, the commander of the French regular troops in North America, Lieutenant-General Louis-Joseph, Marquis de Montcalm, dispatched Levis with 900 men to shore up the western approach. On Isle Royale, Levis ordered a fort built with construction being undertaken by the engineer Captain Jean-Nicolas Desandrouins.

The two vessels would act as the first line of defense for the French on the Upper St. Lawrence River, while the second line of defence would be the fort on Isle Royale. Once past Isle Royale, the St. Lawrence River was plagued with a serious of rapids that made navigation difficult if not dangerous off and on for the next hundred miles or so to Montreal. These rapids, starting with the Galops Rapid near Isle Royale, would act as the third line of defense with the French contesting each rapid.

That same day the French sailors were taken, Gage met with Johnson telling him to stop the Cayugas and others tribes from coming and only to keep a few warriors to act as scouts. Privately Gage finally admitted to Johnson he had given up any idea of proceeding to La Galette.

A scouting party sent out by Johnson returned on September 14 with word that French had destroyed everything at Pointe-au-Baril. They had also delivered Johnson's warning to the Oswegatchies, who sent their thanks to the Indian Superintendent for his care of them and stated they would quit the French interest and show the British the best way to attack Isle Royale which they said was held by less than 600 troops. The Oswegatchies wanted an attack to be made soon fearing the French would re-enforce La Galette should Wolfe be repulsed at Quebec. Johnson quickly forwarded the information to Gage.

At his hut on the 15th, Gage met with Johnson and Colonels Haldimand, Massey and Graham. He asked them how many men would be needed to continue work on the fort at Oswego. The officers figured a little over 1,400 men. That would leave about 1,000 soldiers and an unknown number of warriors, who were constantly arriving, to attack La Galette.

Johnson, ever determined to strike at La Galette, told

Gage that if the French post was destroyed now it would draw off the Oswegatchies from the French interest. Otherwise, Johnson warned, the Oswegatchies might become more firmly attach to the French. An attack on the upper St. Lawrence River French post also would allow the capture of the enemy vessels.

Gage committed to nothing stating that everything depended on Wolfe. He did again tell Johnson he had better stop the Cayugas from coming and send them home. In fact two of Johnson's Indian Department officers, Captain John Lotteridge and Lieutenant William Hare, informed him that the Cayugas were only a day away. They were not the only ones coming to join Johnson in the campaign against La Galette. A number of Onondagas arrived that day with word that the rest of the nation were coming to attack the French even if they had to do it themselves.

Johnson and the three colonels again met with Gage in his hut on the 16th to hear new intelligence gathered from French prisoners. Gage now believed the French were strongly entrenched and outnumbered them and was at loss what do next. He wanted the advice of the officers present, making it clear this was not a council of war.

Massey thought La Galette could be destroyed with "a flying light body of troops" numbering about 500 men.[12] Johnson thought 600 men might take La Galette, which in turn might cause the French to abandon Isle Royale if their

---

[12] *Ibid.*, p. 145.

numbers were weak and were not to learn the true numbers of Gage's attacking force. On the other hand, should the French be too strong they could always retreat. Again Johnson warned that to do nothing might more firmly attach the Oswegatchies to the French interest. Nothing was done, however.

The following day Johnson intended to ask Gage to give him 600 men to attack La Galette as the Indians gathering at Oswego where desirous of it. Johnson believed the Oswegatchies wanted it too. If Gage did not agree, then Johnson meant to ask for his liberty to return home. Neither would happen, at least right away as Johnson continued to stay at Oswego dealing with the warriors still arriving.

About noon on the 30th, an Onondaga party arrived by boat along with Lieutenant Hare and some other whites. Hare and the Onondagas had just turned back a French war party capturing two Indians who they now brought with them. Arriving at Johnson's tent they informed the Indian Superintendent that a priest at La Galette told them there were 2,500 men on Isle Royale fortifying as quick as they could. They also mentioned that a week ago a party of seven men sent out from Amherst had been captured and taken to La Galette with their letters.[13] Johnson passed the information on to Gage.

There was to be no expedition down the Upper St.

---

[13] This party was possibly Captain Tute of the Rangers who set out from Crown Point with nine men, although five would be sent back, with orders from Amherst to scout out Oswegatchie before making contact with Gage. Tute would be exchanged with another 122 prisoners in June of 1760.

Lawrence River in the fall of 1759. Work continued on Fort Ontario and communication was improved with the Mohawk Valley as the campaign season was coming to an end. On October 11, Johnson met with Onondagas, Cayugas, Senecas, Oneidas and Mohawks to thank them on Gage's behalf for their service and discharged them as the general had no other plans then to finish the fort. Any move against the French on the Upper St. Lawrence would have to wait until 1760.

While Amherst was angry at Gage for his inactivity and let him know it, the commander-in-chief had not moved either since reaching Crown Point. The building of the vessels he needed to defeat the little French fleet on Lake Champlain had slowed down due to sawmill problems at Ticonderoga. This was not the only problem delaying him. Amherst was concerned about pushing into Canada until he found more of what was happening with Wolfe at Quebec, which of a letter dated from August 11 did not looking promising.

Attempts to make contact with Wolfe had not gone well. On August 7, a ranger officer set out taking the long journey via the Kennebec River. It would take him almost a month to reach Wolfe. A more direct route was attempted on August 8 by Captain Quinton Kennedy and Lieutenant Archibald Hamilton and a handful of Stockbridge Indians under one of Major Robert Roger's Indian company commanders, Captain Jacob Naunauphtaunk. To help the men pass through enemy territory they carried with them a flag of truce as a pretext of making a peace offer to the Abenakis along their route. It did not work and the men were captured by Abenakis from St. Francis and handed over to the French.

On September 13, Major Robert Rogers and a force of about 200 rangers set off from Crown Point in whaleboats with Amherst orders to attack the Abenaki settlement of St. Francis. Amherst may have been angered over the capture of Kennedy and Hamilton and the supposed violation of their flag of truce, in which Amherst was probably guiltier of, but he other reasons as well. For years St. Francis was the jump off point of numerous raiding parties that swept down on the New England frontier. Rogers meant to bring that to an end. Finally by sending Rogers to strike St. Francis, Amherst could be seen as taking the offence and hopefully at the same time draw French attention from Gage's advance down the St. Lawrence River. Rogers successfully sacked St. Francis and made a harrowing journey home dogged by French and Indian pursuers losing a number of men to starvation and capture along the way.

Amherst finally started north from Crown Point with 4,500 men by water accompanied with the newly built vessels on October 11. His intentions were to destroy the small French fleet on the lake, make a diversion against the French post at Isle-aux-Noix on the Richelieu River, while making a thrust against Montreal. Things started off well enough when three of the enemy vessels were captured, but then the weather turned rough making water travel difficult. On October 18, a boat arrived from Crown Point with important news. Wolfe had captured Quebec about a month earlier, although at the cost of his life. This news changed everything. The army that had been facing Wolfe would now be at Montreal causing Amherst to face stronger opposition then he expected. Amherst decided to turn his army back toward Crown Point. The campaign to capture Canada would have to wait another year.

Sir Jeffery Amherst (Library and Archives Canada).

Chapter 2
The Plan Unfolds: 1760

B y December of 1759 Amherst had been a soldier of the King for 24 years. The son of a prosperous barrister, young Jeffery Amherst was 18 when he donned the King's coat and joined Major-General Sir John Ligonier's Regiment of Horse stationed in Ireland as a cornet. Ligonier was a superb soldier who helped young Amherst, who he called his "dear pupil", in his military career.[14]

Amherst's rank rose in the coming years and he saw service as an aid-de-camp to both Ligonier and the Duke of Cumberland in the War of Austrian Succession, and later acted as commissary for British paid Hessians troops in 1756. This was the same year he was appointed colonel of the 15th Foot. Amherst's big break came at the end of 1757 when the new commander-in-chief, Ligonier who replaced

---

[14] Quoted in C.P. Stacey, 'Jeffery Amherst' *Dictionary of Canadian Biography Vol. IV.*www.biographi.ca.

Cumberland, advanced him from colonel to major-general giving him the task of capturing Louisbourg. Amherst did not let Ligonier down capturing the fortress on July 27, 1758. By November of that year his star ascended even higher when he was appointed the commander-in-chief of British forces in North America after the former commander, James Abercrombie, was recalled for his defeat at Ticonderoga that same year. Now in the last month of 1759 Amherst arrived in the city of New York to begin planning New France's fatal blow.

There was much to be done for the coming campaign as supplies had to be gathered, equipment repaired and troops raised. In January, Amherst was forced to approach the New York Assembly for a loan to cover expenses until money from England arrived. Besides regulars, Amherst needed provincials for the coming campaign and he wrote to the colonial governments requesting the same number of troops they provided in 1759.

The provinces provided the troops, not only out of patriotic duty of ending the war, but also out of necessity. As the colonies that had been in the fighting were heavily in debt and relied upon a reimbursement from England to help them financially, they were in no position to say no to Amherst. By the end of June 14,500 provincial troops from Connecticut, Massachusetts, New York, New Jersey, Rhode Island and New Hampshire would be at Amherst's disposal. Besides white troops, Amherst wanted native help as well and wrote to Johnson in February ordering him to recruit as many Iroquois warriors as he could.

February also saw the official orders arrive from Pitt giving the commander-in-chief in North America a free hand on taking Canada stating that as "your knowledge of the Countries, thro' which the War is to be carried, and from emergent circumstances not to be known here, judge the same to be most expedient."[15]

The plan for the final invasion of Canada would be three pronged. Brigadier-General James Murray with the Quebec garrison was to move up the St. Lawrence River toward Montreal. Brigadier-General William Haviland was to move north from Crown Point, take Isle-aux-Noix and continue up the Richelieu River to Montreal. Finally Amherst would take personal command of the army moving down the Upper St. Lawrence River taking Fort Levis and shooting the rapids before joining with the other two armies in capturing Montreal.

It was a massive plan that would overwhelm Montreal from three sides, but before it got underway, the French struck first.

---

[15] Quoted in Stacey, 'Jeffery Amherst' *Dictionary of Canadian Biography Vol. IV.*www.biographi.ca.

Chapter 3
Desperate Gamble: 1760

Both the governor of New France, Pierre de Rigaud, Marquis de Vaudreuil de Cavagnial[16] and Levis, a capable officer who had seen service in the War of Austrian Succession and had been in North America since 1756 and had taken over the army after Montcalm's death, were in agreement that if New France had any chance of survival Quebec had to be retaken. It was known that the British garrison at Quebec had suffered greatly over the winter and with timely assistance from France the city might be recaptured. If it was, maybe the British would be willing to partake in peace talks instead of launching another expedition against the city?

Success, however, would depend on help from France. In late November 1759, a month or so after the

---

[16] Born in 1698 in New France, Vaudreuil would go on to be governor of Louisiana in 1742. His main goal in life was to be governor of New France which was realized in 1755.

Royal Navy departed Quebec for the winter, French ships managed to slip past the city carrying a message from Levis to France requesting reinforcements, heavy guns, supplies and a naval squadron. Even if help was sent from the mother country, timing was important. The ships from France would have to arrive before the Royal Navy returned to Quebec in the spring. This made the odds of success longer, but no matter, something had to be done before the massive Anglo-American assault got underway.

Vaudreuil distributed a letter to the clergy and militia officers imploring their assistance in getting the militia to turn out for the bold gamble. The governor was not looking for volunteers though, all men fit for duty were ordered to show up or face the threat of death. Besides men, provisions were gathered and stores impressed, while workers were busy building gun carriages and tools.

While these preparations were being made and the bulk of the troops in the colony were readying for the siege of Quebec, New France's western and southern defenses were not neglected. Colonel Louis-Antoine Bougainville, who came to Canada with Moncalm in 1756 as his aide-de-camp, was ordered to take a small detachment of 110 men to Ile-aux-Noix, where 300 men had garrisoned the works over the winter. Work on the island's fortification had been completed in November, the same month Bourlamaque had left the island sick.[17]

---

[17] Work on Isle-aux-Noix progressed slowly when it began in May of 1759 with a small work force until August when Bourlamaque retreated there with about 3,000 men, although the bulk of these men were not actually involved in working on the fort.

Above Brigadier-General Levis (Library and Archives Canada). Below Fort Levis from *A History of St. Lawrence and Franklin*

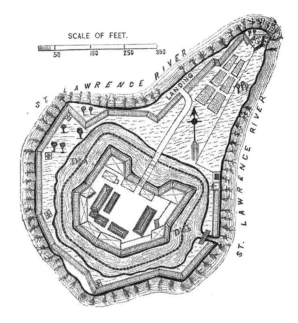

Although Isle-aux-Noix was not impregnable, it could not be ignored either by an advancing army. Both branches of the Richelieu River which flowed around the island, which was located in the middle of the waterway, were barred with chains of big trees linked together at their ends with strong iron rings. These barricades were built to prevent the British from attempting to slip past the island at night. There were no roads that could be used by the British to bypass the island either.

Fort Levis, as the fortification on the rocky little Isle Royale on the Upper St. Lawrence River was named, guarded the western approach to Montreal. Captain Pierre Pouchot was sent to take command of the post after the engineer, Captain Desandrouins, was recalled to aid Levis. Pouchot, a veteran officer who had seen service in Italy, Flanders and Germany and had been in North America since 1754, was no stranger to the Upper St. Lawrence River having had provisional command briefly at Pointe-au-Baril and La Presentation in early 1759.

At that time the main post on the Upper St. Lawrence River was Fort La Presentation where the Oswegatchie River flowed into the St. Lawrence on the south shore. Work on the fort began in 1749 at the site of a small mission which had been there for 31 years. It was a small affair consisting of a small house and barn and later a stockade after the barn had been torched during an Indian raid. The following year the fort was expanded adding more buildings and four timber towers. The fort was good for defense against an Indian attack, but could do little against artillery.

Abbe Francois Picquet, a Sulpician Monk, had recruited a number of Iroquois living south of Lake Ontario who showed an interest to the Christian faith to settle at La Presentation. Picquet planned for the Indians to raise cows and pigs, as well as harvest wild rice, and work the soil. By 1749, six Indians were at the new settlement. It would quickly grow to 396 people two years later. Most of the Iroquois were Onondagas and Cayugas, with a small number of Senecas. By 1754 the village of Oswegatchie consisted of 49 bark cabins.

Further up river about 10 miles from Oswegatchie was Pointe-au-Baril located on the north shore where a shipyard had been constructed in August of 1758. It was protected by an earthwork and a 10-12 foot outer palisade. Two vessels, the *Iroquoise* and the *Outaouaise* were launched from there in 1759.[18]

When Pouchot arrived there in April of that year he found neither vessel completed. He doubled the labourers and ordered work to be pushed on day and night. A third vessel was being built as well, but it was not completed.

The shipyard at Pointe au Baril had been built to replace the loss of Fort Frontenac[19] in August of 1758. That month Lieutenant-Colonel John Bradstreet with a force of 3,000 troops, most of which were Provincials[20] set out

---

[18] The vessels were commanded by Commodore Rene Hypolite Pepin dit La Force and Captain Pierre Boucher de Labroquerie.

[19] Modern Kingston, Ontario.

[20] There were also 157 regulars, 27 artillerymen and 70 Onondagas and Oneidas.

from Oswego and captured the fort on the morning of the August 27.

With word of massive French re-enforcements headed to Fort Frontenac, Bradstreet did not linger long. The fort was destroyed along with 60 cannons. The nine sloops that made up the whole of the French fleet on Lake Ontario were sunk, except two vessels which helped haul away the £35,000 worth of captured goods. Bradstreet then headed back to Oswego having inflicted a staggering blow to the French's western posts and Indian trade as Fort Frontenac had served as their supply base.

Once the *Iroquoise* and the *Outaouaise* at Pointe-au-Baril were complete, Pouchot and 450 men then moved onto Fort Niagara where he took over command there. His time was brief there, surrendering the fort to Johnson on July 25, 1759. Before being sent to New York as a prisoner, Pouchot hosted a dinner for the British officers. In November, Pouchot was exchanged and returned to Montreal.

Now on March 17, 1760, Pouchot set out on the ice for his new command at Fort Levis. Accompanying him was Abbe Picquet and five men with three sleds. Upon taking command at the fort, Pouchot found himself in command of a garrison that consisted of 150 troops, mostly militia, and 180 crew members of the two vessels.

Fort Levis at Pouchot's arrival consisted of a rampart, with the barracks, magazines, officer's quarters, and other buildings inside the works. Pouchot, a military engineer, set his garrison to beefing up the defences. A nine foot timber parapet was constructed upon the original 18 foot wide one and filled with earth brought in from off the island. What was left of the original parapet on the inside now served as a platform for the soldiers to stand on while firing their muskets over the defensive wall. Openings were made in the parapets for the cannons to fire through. On the outside of the parapet was left a four foot wide berm with stakes sharpened and pointing horizontally or obliquely outward from the fort. The rampart was now 11 feet high and better protected the interior of the fort somewhat from the nearby loftier islands of La Magdelaine and La Cuisse.

A gallery was constructed of 14 inch square and 10 foot long pieces of oak logs and was extended along the rampart. Batteries were placed upon the galleries all around the low island. A four foot thick parapet made of earth taken mostly from the bed of the river added to the island's defense ending at the point of the island where a timber redoubt was built and pierced for five cannons. To help stop enemy boats from landing an abatis made of tree branches were placed outside the parapets and extended out into the water. Two places, however, were left on either side of the island allowing friendly boats to land.

Eight cannons without trunnions taken from Fort Frontenac had frames made and were mounted like mortars. In all, Fort Levis boasted 12 12-pounders, 13 4-pounders, 2 8-pounders, 4 1-pounders and 4 6-pounders which were made of brass, while all the other guns were iron. Twelve of these cannons were brought up from Montreal in July.

This little island fort, along with the two vessels and the rapids, was New France's western defense. It was not much and Pouchot's task before him was difficult, especially should Levis fail to retake Quebec.

While Pouchot laboured at Isle Royale, Levis on April 20 boarded his army and 12 old guns on barges and bateaux and headed downriver with an escort of two frigates. Levis had a good size army numbering a little less than 7,000 men, which consisted of eight battalions of regulars strengthened with militia drafts which sometimes outnumbered the regulars themselves, two battalions of Compagnies Franches de la Marine,[21] and a battalion of militia from Montreal. Also accompanying the expedition was a company of cavalry and a contingent of Indians. As the men headed downriver, more militia joined Levis slightly increasing his numbers. The bold gamble to save New France was underway.

---

[21] Called such because they were directed by the Ministry of the Marine which managed the overseas French colonies. It should be noted that the Compagnies Franches de la Marine were independent companies of soldiers raised for duty not only in New France, but Louisiana and other places. They were not sea soldiers such as the Royal Marines.

Chapter 4
Second Siege of Quebec: April-May, 1760

Sometime in the early morning of April 27, a watch on the Royal Navy frigate *Racehorse*, which was docked in Quebec's Lower Town where it had wintered, heard a feeble cry of distress pierce the darkness out on the St. Lawrence River. The ship's captain was quickly informed and he ordered out a boat into the drifting ice. The sailors following the sound of the weak cries found a man on a large piece of ice thoroughly soaked and half dead. With some difficulty they hauled him into the boat and rowed back to the frigate.

Once they got him aboard the ship they revived him and he began to talk. His news was alarming. He was a sergeant with the artillery in Levis's army that had come to retake Quebec. The army was landing above Cap Rouge, about eight miles or so west of Quebec, when the boat the sergeant was in capsized drowning his companions. The sergeant survived by dragging himself up on an ice flow.

Brigadier-General Murray (Library and Archives Canada).

The sergeant was quickly put into a sailor's hammock and carried into Quebec to Brigadier-General Murray's[22] quarters on Mountain Street. After being awoken at 3 a.m., Murray listened to the sergeant's alarming news. Murray had no idea that a sizeable French force was headed his way, thinking from the reports he heard that it was another fighting patrol which had been harassing his troops throughout the winter in a number of bloody skirmishes.

Murray reacted quickly on receiving news of the large French force by leading a large detachment through the mud and snow for the little village of St. Foye located about six miles away to help cover the withdraw of the light infantry posted there. There they found Levis's army who would not attack the British behind their abatis at St. Foy. Instead Levis intended to flank the British that night, but before he could, Murray seeing the danger, demolished the village's church which contained munitions they could not carry off and withdrew back into Quebec.

The next day, Murray led his army back out from Quebec again around 7 a.m. to the Heights of Abraham. To face Levis, Murray had about 3,866 men. This was about half of the 7,000 men Murray had been left with to

---

[22] Born in Scotland in 1721, Murray was a veteran soldier who started his military career in 1736 serving in the Scots brigade of the Dutch Army. Four years later he joined the British army and saw service in the West Indies and Flanders. In 1758 he came to North America and was at the siege of Louisbourg and was with Wolfe at Quebec the next year.

garrison the city when the Royal Navy departed at the end of October the previous year.

The cold winter had been hard on the troops in the shelled out city as many were inadequately dressed such as the 78th Highlanders who were in their kilts. Lack of proper nutrient and diseases such as scurvy, typhus, typhoid, and dysentery had taken their toll on the soldiers killing 1,000 men who could only be temporary buried in snowdrifts till the frost came out of the ground. Another 2,000 or so were unfit for service.

Levis's plan for the 28th was not to fight a battle, but rather to bring up his guns and begin to lay a siege. Considering the enemy was so close and there not being time to fortify the Heights of Abraham, Murray decided "to give the enemy battle before they could establish themselves in consequence".[23]

Reconnoitering ahead of his lines, Murray saw that the main body of the French army was still on the march from St. Foye, although three brigades from the vanguard were in position holding the line Levis meant to occupy. This line consisted of two blockhouses on the right flank, the rising ground in the center, and a mill and fortified windmill on the left. Murray thought this was the time to attack before the French were completely ready, as although their right wing was in position, their left had yet to form. This was the flank he would hit hoping to the

---

23 Quoted in George F. Stanley, *New France: The Last Phase 1744-1760*, (Toronto: McClelland and Stewart, 1968), 246.

drive the French back towards the cliff along the St. Lawrence River were there would be no retreat for them. They would either have to surrender or drown.

Murray's battle line consisted of eight battalions, divided into two brigades with two battalions acting in reserve. Light infantry under Major John Dalling covered Murray's right flank, while the left flank was covered by rangers commanded by Captain Moses Hazen and a 100 volunteer Highlanders, who had been trained during the winter to fight like rangers, under the command of Major Donald MacDonald. With his redcoated battalions drawn up two men deep so as to take up as much room as possible, although there were still large gaps between the battalions, Murray's force moved forward. Being pulled along with the troops were 20 guns and two howitzers.

When they reached the terrain where over seven months earlier Wolfe had drawn his army up, Murray's force stopped and the guns opened up on the French. Levis ordered the troops on the left to fall back and take shelter in nearby Sillery Woods. Murray mistook this move for a retreat and ordered his men to advance further. The troops slogged forward into low ground finding themselves at times in knee deep slush and mud. The guns could no longer be drug any further.

Dalling's light infantrymen furiously attacked the house and windmill held by five companies of French grenadiers driving them back. Dalling's men pursued after them but were themselves attacked by the French troops who had taken cover in Sillery Woods. The light infantrymen were hit hard and those who survived were driven back into the battalions forming the British right flank preventing them from firing on the French who were reforming their ranks. The battered light infantry finally got out of the way and retired to the rear to take no more part in the rest of the battle. The French managed to recapture the house and mill only to be driven out again. Heavy fighting ensued on this flank for the next hour as the 35th Regiment, acting as a reserve, was sent into action to help shore up the British right flank. Casualties began to mount.

Fighting, meanwhile, raged on the British left flank. Here the British took an appalling fire from Canadians in the nearby woods. The French had three guns in the battle, and they now began to open up on the British. Hazen and MacDonald with their rangers and volunteers attacked the two blockhouses and took them, but holding them was another matter. The French counterattacked taking the strong points killing MacDonald and wounding Hazen.

The French superior numbers began to take its toll on the British left flank which had brought up its reserve battalion - the 3rd battalion of the Royal Americans. With both flanks buckling and the center unsteady, Murray ordered a retreat to keep from being cut off from Quebec by Levis. Slogging through the knee deep blood stained snow and slush, the British soldiers made their way back to Quebec leaving behind their guns. The French pursued, but Levis soon called a halt.

The Battle of St. Foye was over and what a bloody day it had been. Murray lost about third of his men: 259 men killed and 829 wounded. Levis's army also suffered as he lost 193 killed and 640 wounded out of about 3,800 troops actually engaged in the fighting.

Murray's battered and bloodied army retreated back into Quebec and prepared for a siege. Levis took the high ground in front of the wall of Quebec and began to build siege lines. Construction was not easy as earth had to be carried in bags by the struggling troops. The task was made more difficult by the British guns firing from Quebec. For two weeks the French and Canadians erected batteries concentrated against the St. Louis Bastion and La Glaciere Bastion along the southern portion of the wall near Cape Diamond.

Finally on May 11, the French guns opened up on the two bastions. The French barrage was not impressive as they had smaller caliber guns than the British and their ammunition was limited. In fact after the initial barrage, Levis ordered his artillerymen to fire only 20 rounds from their four batteries. Murray, on the other hand, had lots of guns and ammunition and made free use of it.

The siege of Quebec now became a waiting game as to whose ships would arrive first - French or British. Actually on May 9, two days before the French guns opened up, a Royal Navy frigate, *Lowestoft,* arrived being two months out of England. Around 9 p.m., on the 15th, three ships appeared. The French could not make out whose they were, but as no message was sent to them and no shots from the British were fired against them it became obvious it was the Royal Navy.

The next morning Levis's army retreated from their lines outside Quebec. The French commander also ordered his bateaux and two frigates upriver. The two ships, *Pomone* and *Atlante* were not to make it. The Royal Navy ships quickly ran *Pomone* ashore while the other French frigate saw the bateaux safely to Cap Rouge. The ship then made it further upriver to Pointe-aux-Trembles where it fought it out with the Royal Navy ships until she ran out of gunpowder. Captain Jean Vauquelin then ordered his ship's mizzen mast chopped down providing an escape route for his crew. Then the captain and his officers surrendered.

The bold gamble to take Quebec was over. It was not surprising the Royal Navy had arrived first. On November 20, 1759, Admiral Sir Edward Hawke and his Royal Navy squadron smashed a French squadron in the battle of Quiberon Bay off the coast of France thwarting any attempt of invading the British Isles. The Royal Navy now controlled the waves being in a position to hamper French seaborne commerce and attempts to aid their oversea colonies.[24] New France was on its own hook.

---

[24] In April the French had sent five transport ships with 400 regulars and a frigate to Canada, but they were not to make it. Three of the transport ships were captured by the Royal Navy blockade while the other ones actually made it to the mouth of the St. Lawrence River but found British ships there first. The French ships then headed for Chaleur Bay and anchored in the Restigouche River (located in modern New Brunswick) where Acadians continued to hold out. There the ships were mostly destroyed by the French themselves when two Royal Navy squadrons moved in on them on July 8.

Major Robert Rogers (Library and Archives Canada).

Chapter 5
A Diversion: May-June, 1760

On May 23, Major Robert Rogers arrived at Albany to meet with Amherst. By 1760 Rogers was a legend. Born in Massachusetts Bay Colony in 1731, Rogers grew up on the New England frontier and was no stranger to French and Indian raids. Hunting and trapping in the wilderness between the English and French settlements had helped hone Rogers's wilderness skills which would be put to good use later in fighting the French and Indians. As a captain of a company of men in Blanchard's New Hampshire Regiment, Rogers came to prominence as a man who was not afraid to venture into French territory in 1755 to gain information on them. By March of the following year, Rogers was commissioned by the then commander-in-chief of British forces in North America and governor of Massachusetts Bay, Major-General William Shirley, as captain of an "Independent Company of

Rangers", later popularly known as Roger's Rangers.[25] Throughout the next four years the Rangers were increased in strength and engaged in numerous scouts, raids and bloody skirmishes with the French and Indian not only on the Lake George/Lake Champlain front, but companies were dispatched to serve in other theatres of operation such as Louisbourg, the 1759 Quebec campaign and the Niagara campaign. The coming campaign of 1760 would be no different.

Amherst had been informed of Levis's siege of Quebec and as yet did not know whose flag fluttered over the city. The general needed Rogers to make a diversion hopefully to draw French troops away from Quebec. The greencoated major was ordered to take 275 rangers and 25 light infantrymen and move down Lake Champlain under the convoy of a brig. Landing on the western shore of the lake, Rogers was to slip past Isle-aux-Noix and hit the posts at St. Jean and Chambly destroying boats, provisions and everything he could. Being careful not to be cut off, they were to make their way back past the east side of Isle-aux-Noix. At the same time 50 rangers were to be sent to attack 'Wigwam Martinique' (Yamaska, Quebec). Rogers was also given a letter to forward to Murray if the major thought best.

Back at Crown Point, Rogers found he did not have enough men to meet the strength ordered by Amherst as Captain Solomon's company of Stockbridge Indians who

[25] John Cuneo, *Robert Rogers of the Rangers*, (Ticonderoga, New York: Ticondergoa Museum, 1988), 33.

were to accompany him had failed to arrive from Albany yet.[26] Rogers had no choice but to make the raid with 250 men. The raiders moved out on June 1 in four sloops which carried the troops and their whaleboats, while a brig acted as an escort.

Two days later one of the sloops sailed off to Missisquoi Bay on the northeastern side of Lake Champlain. Here Lieutenant Robert Holmes and 50 rangers climbed into the lowered whaleboats and made for shore intending to raid 'Wigwam Martinique'. Also going ashore with Holmes were four men who were attempting to take Amherst's letter to Murray at Quebec. The rest of the sloops and brig made for the other side of the lake.

Whaleboats were lowered into the water on June 4. Rogers and the rest of his raiders, about 200 men, climbed aboard and then rowed for the western shore landing about 12 miles south of Isle-aux-Noix. Two sloops attached to Rogers were to sail further down the lake closer to the French fort intending to draw their attention while the rangers slipped past it. However, Rogers didn't move as a heavy rain pounded down on the 5th. That afternoon two French vessels made their appearance and were spotted by the sloops as well as the rangers. Figuring the French would watch the sloops all night, Rogers ordered the vessels to return and join the rest of the Royal Navy vessels waiting at Isle la Motte.

Despite this, the damage was already done. The

---

[26] Throughout the war at various times Rogers had Indian companies attached to his rangers.

French had spotted where Rogers and his men had gone ashore. Scouts who had been watching Isle-aux-Noix returned with more bad news. The French had sent 350 men from Isle-aux-Noix to the west side of Lake Champlain with intentions of cutting Rogers off. He soon learned that the French were only about a mile away.

Although outnumbered, Rogers meant to fight. He anchored his right flank against a bog and expected the attack to fall on his left flank which it did around 11:30 a.m.. Rogers had a surprise for his attackers. Lieutenant Jacob Farrington with 70 rangers moved through the bog and hit the French in the rear. Rogers then attacked their front. The French broke and retreated back into a thick cedar swamp with the rangers in hot pursuit. The French then attempted to escape by scattering into small parties. By this time the rain was pounding down again and pursuit was called off. The sharp three hour engagement had cost Rogers 17 men killed and 10 wounded.[27] The French lost about 32 killed and 19 wounded.

With the dead and wounded placed in the boats, Rogers and men rowed to Isle la Motte to join the vessels there. Rogers ordered a ship to Crown Point with a report he wrote to Amherst describing what had happened so far. Then after the dead were buried on the island, Rogers prepared to continue with the raid. Fortunately his numbers were increased when 25 Stockbridge Indians and 30 light infantrymen from the 17th Regiment arrived.

[27] The number of killed would rise to 18 when one of Roger's officer shortly succumbed to his wounds.

His new plan called for the vessels to sail to Windmill Point at the entrance of the Richelieu River. They were to divert the French at Isle-aux-Noix while Rogers and his men landed at the mouth of the Chazy River. If the raid went well, Rogers planned to be picked up on the east shore of Lake Champlain at Windmill Point or near it. Rogers, however, figured he would be attacked and if things went bad for him, he planned to retreat back to the west side of the lake to a place between Isle la Motte and the battleground of the 6th. In either case Rogers would signal the ships by smoke and three guns fired "at a minute's interval each from the other, and repeated a second time, in half an hour after the first".[28]

About midnight on June 9, Rogers and 220 men came ashore on their planned landing spot and immediately made for Fort St. Jean as fast as possible. The Rangers made it past Isle-aux-Noix undetected and continued north reaching the road that lead from St. Jean to Montreal on the evening of June 15. At 11:00 p.m. that night Rogers headed for Fort St. Jean with the intention of attacking it, but 400 yards from the fort the raiders held up. After scouting the fort, Rogers determined it was impossible to take by surprise as it was well guarded and made more difficult by the fact that major was spotted and fired upon.

---

[28] Robert Rogers, *The Annotated and Illustrated Journals of Major Robert Rogers*, Edited by Timothy J. Todish, (Fleichmanns, New York: Purple Mountain Press, 2002), 201.

Not wasting any time on making an attempt against St. Jean, Rogers headed down the Richelieu River three miles for Fort St. Therese reaching it at 2 a.m.. After reconnoitering the place at daybreak, Rogers discovered the place consisted of a stockade around two large storehouses with another 15 houses outside. Watching the enemy haul hay into the fort, Rogers had a daring plan for taking it.

When a cart full of hay entered the fort's gateway, Rogers and his men charged the fort and houses catching the French by surprise. The Rangers were in the fort before the cart could be moved and the gate shut. Not a shot was fired and no one was hurt. Rogers bagged 24 enemy soldiers and 78 inhabitants as prisoner, although some young men made their escape north to Fort Chambly.

After examining the prisoners Rogers determined he could not take Fort Chambly now that they had been warned. The raiders torched the fort, hay and houses. Cattle, horses, wagons and all but eight boats were destroyed as well. The women and children were sent towards Montreal. Then with the 26 male prisoners, Rogers and his men crossed the river in the captured eight boats, which were then promptly destroyed. Rogers now quickly headed south for the east shore of Lake Champlain.

By this time the French from Isle-aux-Noix were out looking for him. Roger's advance guard soon collided with the advance guard of 800 enemy soldiers on June 20.

Fortunately the main body of French soldiers were a mile behind their advance guard, giving Roger's advance guard time to retreat. The raiders now moved with all possible speed reaching the eastern shore and sending the pre-arranged signal. The vessels arrived and not too soon. As the raiders were climbing aboard, the French appeared only to watch Rogers and his men escape.

The following day, Rogers picked up Lieutenant Holmes and his detachment who had failed to find 'Wigwam Martinique'. Two days later the raiders were back at Crown Point. The French had not seen the last of him as Rogers and his rangers would be back in the coming months, only this time it would not be a raid.

Chapter 6
Securing Indian Help: March-July, 1760

As preparations were underway for the conquest of New France, Sir William Johnson worked hard to recruit warriors for the coming campaign and draw Indians away from the French. Writing from Fort Johnson on March 7, Johnson informed Amherst that two Oswegatchies had told the Superintendent the great part of their people intended to leave Oswegatchie and "come amongst the Six Nations in the spring." Johnson admitted that he did not believe the "seeming good disposition" of the Oswegatchies proceeded from "any real regard for us, but from the low circumstances of the enemy, and their own distresses." Johnson reassured Amherst he would recruit as many warriors friendly to the British as he could, while not neglecting to attempt "withdrawing as many

Indians from the French" as possible.[29]

In fact Johnson had been visited not only by the Oswegatchies, but other Canadian Iroquois as well who had a settlement along the St. Lawrence River at Akwesasne (also called St. Regis), about 50 miles downriver from Oswegatchie, and two settlements near Montreal.[30]

To arm, cloth and acquire all the other supplies he needed for the warriors he recruited, Johnson requested £5,000 from Amherst. Although it was a goodly sum, Johnson wrote that is was unavoidable as large numbers of people from several nations were in a famished condition due to failure of their corn crops.

Nine days later Amherst approved the money, but added that as the military chest was so low at the present time, he asked Johnson if he could obtain credit for some time. As for the Indians allied to the French, Amherst warned that if they continued in their attachment to the enemy "they must take the consequence that will ensue from a continuance of war" which the commander-in-chief was determined to vigorously pursue ending with "the entire reduction of Canada."[31]

---

[29] William L. Stone, *The Life of Sir William Johnson, Bart.* Vol. II, (Albany: J. Munsell, 1865), 122.

[30] The Canadian Iroquois consisted of the Oswegatchies, Akwesasnes, Kanesetakes and Kahnawakes who were named after the communities they resided in. These tribes were all originally of the Six Nations who had moved to Canada because of their conversion to Catholicism. These four tribes were also numbered among the Seven Nations of Canada which included Abenakis of St. Francis and the Algonquins and Nipissings who lived in the same village as the Kanesetakes and finally the Hurons of Lorette

[31] Stone, *Johnson*, 123-124.

While Johnson attempted to draw the Oswegatchies and other Canadian Iroquois tribes and their allies away from the French, Pouchot at Fort Levis endeavored to retain them. He advised them not to attend a council they were invited to in an Onondaga village. Pouchot also kept his eye on the British. On April 1, he dispatched an Oswegatchie chief named Charles to Oswego posing as a hunter coming to trade. To add more credibility to Charles's story, Pouchot gave him some pelts.

Arriving at Oswego, Charles was met by an interpreter and asked what he wanted. He stated that he had been hunting and wished to trade before heading back to Oswegatchie. Oswego's commander was suspicious of Charles true motives and would not allow him into the new fort. Instead the officer informed Charles of a great council that was going to be held at Oswego and of a great army that would be assembling to take Montreal. The British knew of Fort Levis, but the commandant said they would pass it "like a beaver's hut".[32]

After holding their own council, the Oswegatchies decided to send an envoy to the Onondagas asking them whether they continued to regard them as relatives or not. The envoy was also to inform the Onondagas that they had no intentions of leaving Oswegatchie where they had been instructed in the Catholic faith. As proof of their determination to remain at their home along the St. Lawrence River, they intended to plant their fields with

[32] M. Pouchot, *Memoir Upon the Late War in North America between France and England 1755-1760 Vol. 1.,* Franklin B. Hough (editor and translator) ,(Roxbury, Mass.: W. Elliot Woodward, 1866) p. 247.

crops as normal and if need be defend themselves against any disturbance.

Despite their tough talk, an Oswegatchie chief attempted to dissuade Pouchot from sending out a party of Mississaugas he had just equipped on April 28 for fear they would provoke the British into coming and attacking them. Pouchot attempted to ease his fears by stating the Mississaugas had nothing to do with them and had set out on their own account.

Six days later two Mississaugas reported to Pouchot that the English had constructed a large 18 gun vessel at Fort Niagara and were planning to build a bigger one. More reports arrived on May 7 that the British were beginning to assemble troops at Fort Stanwix. It was also reported that Johnson was planning on holding a great council.

More ominous news arrived on May 14, when an Onondaga sent word to the Oswegatchies that they needn't bother planting crops this year as the English would destroy everything when they came. He advised the Oswegatchies that if they did not wish to die they should move to Toniata,[33] which was an island above Isle Royale.

The Oswegatchies took this threat seriously with five families moving to Toniata where they ran up the English flag as an added security measure. On May 18, Pouchot held a council with the chiefs and women of Oswegatchie trying to get them to bring back the people who had moved to the island. The council had contemplated

---

[33] Modern Grenadier Island.

rooting out those from the island and making them go to nearby Isle Piquet where a mission had been established.

In the end it was decided those who didn't wish to come back were free to do as they liked, but they would not be considered part of the village anymore. The families at Toniata returned and gave up the English flag. Clearly the Oswegatchie were concerned about the imminent British campaign and their well being. The growing tension was not going to let up any time soon as reports from Indian scouts and prisoners spoke of the British troop built up at Oswego.

While Pouchot had Indians reporting on the British at Oswego, the British in turn had Indians reporting on Fort Levis. One such Iroquois, who had belonged to the mission at La Presentation, arrived from Oswego to learn what was going on at Fort Levis. He at the same told Pouchot that the army at Oswego was to number 12,000 men and would come and batter Fort Levis.

This Iroquois was not the only Indian sent by the British. A small eight man war party made up of Senecas, Mohawks, Onondagas, Mississaugas, and a white man named George McMickling had an encounter with an Oswegatchie chief and some women in a canoe on the Oswegatchie River. The chief warned them that they were "all dead men" if they did not retire as they were close to a French post and had been discovered. The pro-British Indians took the chief's advice but not before they exchanged some information on the French failed attempt to retake Quebec; the whereabouts of the Ottawas and other war parties on the prowl; and finally British troop movement.[34]

A pro-French war party brought in two prisoners they had painted and dressed like Indians. They were a militia captain and his brother from the Mohawk Valley who were of particular interest to Pouchot as he stayed in their house when he was a prisoner being taken to New York. They had not treated him well, but fortunately for them Pouchot did not return the favour. The tall prisoners were made to do the common dance of the slaves, but were spared the running of the gauntlet by being taken directly to Fort Levis instead of Oswegatchie. From the prisoners Pouchot learned that Amherst commanded the army that was daily passing through the Mohawk Valley towards Oswego and was to number 11,000 men. More news reached Pouchot from Indian scouts making similar reports.

With only 300 men or so on the Upper St. Lawrence River, Pouchot was in a tough situation. The loyalty of the local Indians was quickly slipping away as they saw to their own survival. Pouchot would only have the walls of Fort Levis to take on a massive Anglo-American army which was assembling. He could not stop the army, but maybe he could buy Levis time. Levis would write: "We shall be fortunate if the enemy amuse themselves with capturing it [Fort Levis]. My chief anxiety is lest Amherst should reach Montreal so soon that we may not have time to unite our

---

[34] Pouchot, *Memoirs Upon the Late War,* 256.

forces to attack Haviland or Murray."[35]

To watch Murray on the St. Lawrence River above Quebec 300 troops were stationed at Pointe-aux-Tremble, with another 200 at Jacques Cartier and finally 1,200 men at Deschambault under Jean-Daniel Dumas. At Isle-aux-Noix, Bougainville had 1,450 soldiers, while another 1,200 to 1,500 were a few miles away at St. Jean. There was also assistance from various Indian tribes, although this was quickly vanishing. New France's last grasp of survival lay in Levis being able to defeat the Anglo-American armies piecemeal.

---

[35] Quoted in Francis Parkman, *Moncalm and Wolfe,* (New York: Collier Books, 1962) 595.

Chapter 7
Assembling Armies: May-June, 1760

Albany was a hub of activity in the late spring. Here was the first place of assembly for two of the three armies that would drive on Montreal from Crown Point and Oswego. Massing troops for both those places took time. Some of this delay was caused by the provincials, which made up a large portion of these forces, who were slow on making their way up the Hudson River to Albany.

The provincials, along with the British regulars, while camped near Albany were trained in regular and irregular warfare, exercised in firing ball and were "trained up in every particular that prudence, with experience, could dictate, to render the troops expert in an open or covered country."[36] By 1760, the British army knew a thing or two

---

[36] Captain John Knox, *An Historical Journal of the Campaigns in North America Vol. II.,* (Toronto: The Champlain Society, 1914) 529

about fighting in the forests of North America.

Besides training, an added precaution was taken when an order was issued to the provincial regiments to make a return of any Swiss or Frenchmen serving in their companies. If there were any Swiss or Frenchmen they were to state whether they had been on other campaigns or if this was their first one. The commanding officers were to check up on the men to make sure their information was accurate.

The Massachusetts, Rhode Island and New Hampshire provincials were assigned to accompany Haviland.[37] From Albany or nearby Greenbush the troops would proceed north for Crown Point. Captain Samuel Jenks, a blacksmith by trade, but now in command of a Massachusetts company of provincials, for example, was ordered on May 30 to take 50 men and a number of bateaux loaded with provisions up the Hudson River to Fort Miller. Supplies and boats then had to be hauled by wagons half a mile across land, before Jenks could continue with his company to Fort Edward by water.

By June 10, he and his men had marched 15 miles or so to Fort George, located at the southern end of Lake George. The next day they started out by bateaux for Ticonderoga.

At this place on June 15, Jenks and his men were issued muskets, as up to this point they had been unarmed, and set off for Crown Point. They arrived there

[37] Born in Ireland in 1718, Haviland began his military career in 1739. He arrived in North America in 1757 and would see action at Fort Ticonderoga and accompany Amherst on Lake Champlain in 1759.

Above A West View of Oswego and Fort Ontario (Library of Congress).

Below A South View of Crown Point (Library of Congress).

the next day. Here Haviland was assembling his invading force of regulars and provincials. Many more New England provincials would be following Jenks north.

The New York, Connecticut and New Jersey provincials, meanwhile, were dispatched west to Oswego. Supplies had to be sent as well. Colonel Nathaniel Woodhull's 3rd Regiment of New York Provincials, for example, broke camp on June 11 and marched to Schenectady while their camp equipage and baggage were moved by wagons overseen by Colonel John Bradstreet. The officers were under orders not to bring any chests or boxes which were unnecessary and just took up valuable space. At Schenectady the troops and equipment were put on 52 bateaux and headed up the Mohawk River carrying with them 800 barrels of provisions.

Besides provincials, regular and rangers were also dispatched the roughly 260 mile journey from Albany to Oswego. Troops, artillery and provisions heading up the Mohawk River would be forced to portage at the Great Carrying Place to Wood Creek.[38]

Robert Kirkwood, a soldier with the 77th Highland Regiment, would recount how the creek was very low forcing the provincials to drag their bateaux through about four inches of water. This low water greatly slowed down the movement of troops. Two years earlier a soldier passing through with Bradstreet mentioned the use of dams here. Water was allowed to build up then the sluice

---

[38] Also called Oneida Carry. Fort Stanwix was built in 1758 to replace smaller earlier forts to protect this vital portage.

was opened allowing the boats to float down to the next dam. There the process was repeated. From Wood Creek the troops and supplies would then enter Oneida Lake and finally onto the Oswego River. There another portage was required to get around the falls. Finally the river was followed to Lake Ontario where Oswego would be reached.

Besides bateaux, whaleboats were also sent up the Mohawk River and then onto Oswego rowed by New Jersey troops and some New York provincials. The troops handling these sturdy and easily maneuverable boats were ordered only take their arms, provisions and blankets. Provisions were to move by bateaux only.

On June 19, Amherst set out on the journey himself arriving at Oswego on July 9. That same day the two French vessels were spotted not far from Oswego, but not for long. As the two British snows[39] under Captain Loring were expected at any hour, bateaux were sent out to decoy the French into intercepting them. The French vessels show no interested in the bateaux and sailed away.

The troops that were arriving at Oswego were put to work clearing ground for an encampment and constructing sheds for hospitals. To protect the camp, the two ranger companies under Captain Amos Ogden and Joseph Waite[40]

---

[39] A type of brig.

[40] Both men were tough ranger officers who the previous year had accompanied Rogers on his St. Francis Raid. Ogden, who had been seriously wounded in the raid, raised a company of rangers from New Jersey being given $500 bounty money from Amherst in March of 1760.

established an advanced post where they kept up daily patrols.

On the 14th, the two British vessels finally arrived and were sent off that night in search of the French vessels. The next day a ranger captain and 15 rangers from each company set out in whaleboats to assist Loring by acting as decoys. So far Loring had little luck in engaging the French vessels as they were spotted at Oswego on the 20th. Amherst dispatched three whaleboats to warn Loring and have him station his vessels to prevent the French from re-entering the St. Lawrence.

The following day Captain Samuel Willyamos and 134 men from the Royal Americans were sent to one of the islands with provisions for Loring. By the 27th, Loring was back at Oswego unsuccessful in preventing the French vessels from re-entering the St. Lawrence River and also unsuccessful in finding the island where Willyamos was posted. An officer and eight of Ogden's rangers were quickly sent off to warn Willyamos that Loring had returned to Oswego as the detachment of Royal Americans were now vulnerable to an attack by the French vessels if they returned and found them.

Work, meanwhile, continued on Fort Ontario. Orders were given on July 27 that the regiments would provide three reliefs for the fort as work must continue all day. The first relief was to work until 10 a.m., the second relief until 3 p.m., and the last relief until 8 p.m.

On July 29, Amherst sent a letter to Haviland to begin his advance down Lake Champlain on August 10, about the same time he intended to set off himself.

Haviland had been gathering his force at Crown Point since about mid-June. While men, provisions and supplies were moved up from Albany, work continued on the works at Crown Point. A small pox hospital was set up away from the main camps. This dreaded disease had caused some trouble earlier in Albany. A handful of provincials who already had small pox were ordered to ply between the hospital and the camps by bateau. To prevent the spread of the disease they were under the strict order not to enter the camps, but to take their instructions from the doctor of the hospital.

Alarm spread through the camps around Crown Point on July 8 when an estimated 300 French raiders and a handful of Indians struck a work party of rangers outside their camp on the east side of Lake Champlain. One ranger was killed and six wounded, four of which were expected to die. Major Rogers immediately took after them with his rangers. Rogers returned the next day without having caught up with the enemy.

While Amherst was writing to Haviland about launching his advance at the end of July, the third prong in Amherst's plan to conquer New France had been in motion for a little over two weeks.

Chapter 8
Murray's Advance: July-September, 1760

Murray's hold on Quebec was strengthened with the arrival of supply ships, frigates and ships of the line not long after Levis's retreat in early May. In the coming weeks the sick troops at Quebec began to improve when they were moved to the Island of Orleans where fresh air and fresh provisions did wonders for their health. A number of recuperated troops arrived from New York and other places allowing Murray to have 2,451 troops when he began his advance up the St. Lawrence River.

His army was divided into two brigades, with the right one commanded by Colonel Ralph Burton and the left brigade commanded by Colonel William Howe.

Burton's Brigade consisted of four battalions: the 1st Battalion of Grenadiers drawn from grenadier companies of the 15th, 35th, 47th, 58th Regiments, and the 3rd Battalion of the Royal Americans; the 1st Battalion consisted of the 15th and 48th Regiments; the 3rd Battalion made up of the 35th Regiment and the 3rd Battalion of the Royal Americans; while the 5th Battalion consisted of the 47th and 78th Regiments.

Howe's Brigade consisted of three battalions: the 2nd Battalion of Grenadiers drawn from the grenadiers companies of the 28th, 43rd, 48th, 78th Regiments, and the 2nd Battalion of the Royal Americans; the 4th Battalion made up of the 43rd Regiment and the 2nd Battalion of the Royal Americans; while finally the 2nd Battalion consisted of the 28th and 58th Regiments.

Also accompanying the expedition were a detachment of rangers and royal artillery, as well a large number of sailors and bateaumen to man the 32 vessels, nine floating batteries and numerous flat-bottomed boats and bateaux needed to get the army upriver.

The soldiers' baggage were loaded on the vessels on July 11. The following day Murray reviewed his little army, and on the 13th the soldiers boarded their transports. Boarding one of the ships was Lieutenant John Knox of the 43rd who would leave a vivid account of the expedition upriver. Much of what follows is drawn from his work.

Not being able to wait any longer for two regiments expected from Louisbourg, Murray prepared to set out believing Amherst was already in motion. Leaving over 3,000 troops to garrison Quebec of which 1,700 were fit for duty, the rest being sick and convalescents, Murray's flotilla set sail at 3 p.m. on the 14th. Word was left for the

Louisbourg troops to be sent upriver as soon as they arrived.

Murray told Pitt his intentions in a letter written the day before adding that the moment he arrived at Montreal he should probably be master of the whole country. Murray figured Levis would have to assemble his force to defend Montreal and if the Canadians did not join him, the French commander's force would not greatly outnumber his. If the Canadians did join Levis, then their country would be abandoned and left to Murray's mercy. As Murray could travel four times faster by water than could the Canadians by land, he reckoned it would be impossible for them to save their harvest if they took up arms against him.

On the 15th, Murray's fleet weighed anchor and set sail at 4:15 a.m., with a favorable wind passing Point au Tremble an hour and fifteen minutes later. By 7:30 a.m., they passed the French works at Jacques Cartier. The garrison fired a few shots at the passing fleet, but as the river was wide no harm was done. No attempt was made to take the works at Jacques Cartier as the fleet sailed on upriver anchoring near the village of Deschambault around 9 a.m.. Ahead was spotted two vessels "of an uncommon construction" under Dutch colors with white jacks who cleared off at the sight of Murray's fleet.[41]

That evening at low water, boats were sent out to sound out the rapids in the channel. The British found the depth varied from six feet to thirty-six feet with navigation

---

[41]Knox, *Journal*, 468.

64

being difficult as the river was not only shallow, but full of rocks peeking above the water's surface. The tide, however, would bring the river up here nine feet.

The following morning at 7 a.m., the *Porcupine* and part of the fleet weighed anchor and attempted to make it through the rapids. An hour later a French battery of three guns situated near a church fired on them, while the two French vessels spotted the day before opened up as well. These vessels were soon driven off by the British floating batteries.

While the *Porcupine*, a sloop, and other armed vessels returned cannon fire with the French, the troop transports headed through the rapids. Two of these transports ran aground, but as the tide was up managed to get free with no damage. The exchange of cannon fire had cost the British four men killed from the 78th with another few wounded.

Only part of the fleet managed to get past the rapids with the tide. The other part was forced to anchor below the rapids and wait for the tide to return. That evening the rapids were again sounded and the floating batteries and flat-bottomed boats moved down river to join the portion of the fleet anchored below the rapids.

About night fall two companies of grenadiers moved down river to scout out the garrison at Jacques Cartier hoping that the French had sent most of their troops to watch the fleet leaving the works there undermanned. After the grenadiers discovered Jacques Cartier was strongly garrisoned they returned to the fleet.[42]

While the grenadiers were scouting out Jacques Cartier, the fleet became alarmed late that same night by a large fire made by the French. More signal fires flickered in the darkness on both sides of the river.

The following morning three floating batteries pounded away at the nearby French camp for an hour forcing them to change their position. At night fall nine officers and 200 regulars, along with an officer and 50 rangers slipped into boats with orders to move down river about nine miles and land on the south side of the river. There half the regulars were to be posted in a house while the other half would act as a covering party for the rangers who were to surprise and rout French regulars positioned opposite the fleet below the rapids. They were then to return to their ships.

At around 10 p.m., the regulars and rangers moved down river attempting to land at the parish of St. Croix when they ran into trouble. The boats grounded on a bar of sand causing the men to jump out into a foot of water. As they waded to shore they soon discovered the water got deeper reaching up to their waists. Fortunately they had taken precautions to keep their ammunition dry.

Once they waded onto shore they found the terrain steep and thickly covered with fallen trees making climbing impossible. The troops had no choice but to make

---

[42] On September 10, the 50 French regulars and 150 Canadian militia holding out at Fort Jacques Cartier surrendered to 700 British troops from Quebec.

their way half a mile along the shore until they found a place where they could climb up the rugged hill to the summit. Once they finally moved inland, the soldiers found a farm house where a detachment of the regulars were posted. The rangers and covering party quickly set out to find the enemy troops.

The Canadian inhabitants, meanwhile, abandoned their homes and took to the woods. At daylight some showed themselves along the edge of the woods. They made no effort to surrender despite the efforts of the posted regulars to get them to do. As they made no resistance no harm was done to them.

The rangers at day break got a view of about 40 enemy soldiers and soon informed the captain of the covering party. After a plan was decided upon the regulars in the covering party were divided into two parties, one taking position along a road above the French, and the other on the road below them. The rangers, meanwhile, seized the high ground behind the French and then rushed down and fired on them. The French soldiers caught by surprise managed to return fire and then attempted to escape. They soon found themselves trapped by the divided covering party and were all either killed, wounded or captured. The regulars and rangers soon made signals to be picked up and made their way back to their ships with their prisoners.

Murray's fleet was still held up at the rapids. The delay was not all bad as an enemy supply bateau was captured bagging the British a supply of meal, barley and flour. Meanwhile, the rangers and grenadiers took a twenty mile circuit throughout the countryside where they found many inhabitants, some of whom delivered up their arms stating they hoped the war would be over soon in the British favor so they could remain in peace. A trade developed between these people who gave the soldiers milk, butter and eggs in exchange for salt pork.

On the 19th, contrary winds kept the fleet from moving. That same day the entire parish of St. Croix surrendered and gave up their arms. Wind kept the fleet from advancing any distance the following day. Murray went ashore that day with the rangers and a company of light infantry and headed several miles up country where he spoke with some of the people reminding them they cannot fight a war without ships, artillery and ammunition. As they and their harvest were at Murray's mercy, he implored them to consider their own interest and not to provoke him anymore.

Murray then turned on a priest and warned the clergy to preach the Gospel, but not to interfere with military matters or in the quarrel between the British and French. A number of Canadians took the oath of neutrality. In the coming days and weeks more Canadians would do the same.

On the 23rd, Murray received intelligence that a party of Indians were sent to the south side of the river to annoy and pick off his men. Murray sent a flag of truce to Dumas at Deschambault warning him that if the Indians were not recalled, or if any barbarities were committed against his troops, no quarter would be given to French regulars or others captured. Despite Murray's warning, intelligence came in that four bateaux load of Indians crossed over the river to the south side.

A sergeant in the French regulars was captured the next day on the south side of the river disguised in the garb of a Canadian. Accused of being a spy he was sentenced to hang and taken to a tree to have his neck stretched. Not wanting to swing, the spy spoke freely about the French forces facing the British upriver which he stated amounted to about 400 men from Trois-Rivieres to Quebec. Two battalion of regulars and body of Canadians and Indians were posted at Isle Royale, Isle-aux-Noix and Isle Galot; while the rest of the French forces were situated between Trois-Rivieres and Montreal. Upon the first signal these troops were to retire to the island of Montreal for their final stand. He added that there was not much artillery at Montreal, only some brass field-pieces taken at St. Foye. Trois-Rivieres, he added, was only held with about 30 men and six cannons and one mortar. More news on the enemy arrived when a deserter from Montreal brought word that French soldiers were greatly dissatisfied and mutinous, while the Canadians were abandoning their posts.

On July 26, the rapids were finally passed by the rest of the fleet without incident or fire from the French. Two armed boats were sent on upriver to Trois-Rivieres to sound out the depth there. Being close to the south shore the boat crew exchanged words with a body of Canadians nearby warning them if they bothered the ships they would blast them and their houses to pieces. Troops would be then landed and their country would be destroyed. What the crewmen took to be an officer replied that they would not annoy them and should their officers come ashore he would personally see they would be unharmed. Two canoes full of greens were sent out to the British boats to mark the Canadian's sincerity.

The fleet continued upriver the following day where they met more Canadians who were not as hospitable. The floating batteries and armed sloop fired their cannons on a body of Canadians assembling in a hostile manner not far from a church for half an hour. The Canadians charged down closer to the vessels and returned fire with their muskets and then retired. They did this again, but after a shot from one of the vessels killed a man and wounded two others, the Canadians ceased such action.

Although New France's defenders would offer little resistance or trouble to Murray's fleet, the river would. The *Porcupine* became grounded about a three miles downriver from Trois-Rivieres. Fortunately, the transport ships and the *Duke*, a 350 ton vessel, missed the shoal. The anchor of the *Porcupine* was rowed quite a distance from the sloop and dropped into the river. The vessel then attempted to warp herself off the shoal to no avail as the cable broke. She was stuck, at least for the day.

On August 1, the *Porcupine* attempted to warp herself a second time, but again broke a cable. After the guns and part of her ballast were removed, the *Porcupine* was towed into deep water. Fortunately no damage was done to the sloop as she had been grounded on loose sand.

Two days later, Murray, Burton and Howe headed upriver to reconnoiter Trois-Rivieres where it was thought that Bourlamaque was there with 6,000 men. At 4 p.m. on the 4th, the fleet sailed closer to Trois-Rivieres anchoring near the south shore. A little skirmish around 10 p.m. flared up when a British vessel attempted to capture a French sloop but was forced off after being discovered.

On the south side of the river the Canadians came to the fleet supplying them with poultry, eggs and vegetables in exchange for salt pork and beef. Meanwhile, across the river at Trois-Rivieres the French were busy improving their defensive positions.

The situation was looking grim for the French. The troops from Deschambault had been following the British fleet along the north bank but had no means of stopping them. Entrenchments were being built on the islands at the opening of Lake St. Peter, but as there were several channels and they had no artillery or powder, the French at best could only slow Murray's advance. "We are at the very crisis of our fate," admitted Levis in a letter written to Marechal de Belleisle, the minister of war, on August 7. Levis would go onto confess that they would make every effort to save the colony, but their situation was so unfortunate that miracles were needed to do it. At the very least if they could not save New France they would "save the honour of the King's arms."[26]

---

[26] Knox, *Journal*, 484-486.

Trois-Rivieres in 1810 (Library and Archives Canada).

On the 8th, the fleet sailed past Trois-Rivieres, with the floating batteries positioning themselves to cover the passage of the convoy. With a telescope to his eye, John Knox aboard the passing fleet spotted about 2000 enemy troops, mostly French regulars and a few Canadians lining the works along with about 50 warriors painted a reddish hue with their faces being a different color. He also spotted enemy light cavalry. The fleet sailed past without incident with the French troops being able to do little but file after them along the north bank.

The river again proved more a hindrance then the French as some of the fleet became grounded, forcing them to be lightened before they could get moving again. August 9 saw the river causing more trouble as the larger ships plowed through the soft sand and slime muddying the water in their wake. The *Porcupine* again grounded bringing the fleet to a halt.

The following day several of the ships were forced to

warp themselves upriver out of the shallow water. The *Porcupine*, meanwhile, had to off load her guns and part of her ballast unto boats drawing less water to get free.

A wet foggy morning on the 11th delayed a detachment of grenadiers and light troops under Major Agnew from setting out for St. Francis, where they were to get fresh provisions and send off a party of rangers to make contact with Haviland. It was between 11 a.m. and noon when the troops began to row for their objective. Around 2 p.m., they made the entrance of the St. Francis River. Here the boats were ordered to halt, while Major Agnew moved ahead to reconnoiter.

A large number of French then appeared on the edge of the woods which carpeted each side of the St. Francis River. Agnew had been ordered by Murray not to make a descent up the St. Francis River if the enemy could cut him off. After viewing the French for some time, Agnew ordered the boats back to their ships. The fleet then moved on.

Pushing further upriver, the fleet cleared Lake St Peter and followed the river channel into a group of islands. Around 9 a.m., the fleet came to a halt when they discovered at boom blocking their passage. For three hours sailors worked at cutting away the 16 inch cable. By noon the fleet was underway again reaching Sorel between 6 and 7 p.m.. It was discovered that the French had established a post at the left side of the mouth of the Richelieu River to thwart a junction with Haviland.

The fleet moved a little further upriver where it

anchored. A British deserter from the previous year now surrendered to a detachment sent ashore to get provisions. From him it was learned that Bourlamaque with two battalions of regulars and a body of militia were at Sorel.

By 3 p.m. on the 13th, the *Porcupine* with part of the fleet and the floating batteries was back at the mouth of the Richelieu River. The rest of the fleet soon joined them when it was reported that the French were sending a frigate, a couple of other vessels, and several floating batteries to attack Murray's fleet. No attack ever materialized.

Montreal now lay only 40 miles way or so from where Murray was anchored. Attempting to make contact with Haviland, five rangers slipped away from the fleet and made their way through the French lines heading south with orders to find the army coming north from Crown Point.

On the 14th, the 1st Battalion of Grenadiers, the rangers, and 500 other troops landed on the island of Ignatius which abounded in corn, cattle and poultry. Here the redcoated troops and greencoated rangers only found women and children as the men had left their homes to join the enemy. By the afternoon, part of the troops were rowing back to the ships when someone said they spotted a large body of French troops flanked by Canadian militia on the far end of the island. The boats were quickly called back. The British troops marched to the high ground and formed for battle. At the same time an express was quickly sent to Murray.

Major Agnew leading the grenadiers and rangers made an excursion around the island picking up a large number of sailors and disorderly redcoats who were plundering the inhabitants. It was then discovered there was no French soldiers on the island. The alarm had been caused by sailors shooting some of the inhabitant's horses.

By this time Murray had arrived only to be told it was a false alarm. The troops climbed back into their boats and pushed off for their respective ships. Murray was not happy and the next day a stern warning was issued that if any soldier was caught plundering or "offering any violence to the women of the island" they would be instantly hanged.[43] A similar warning was issued to the sailors.

On the 16th, all the troops were to land on the island so the transport ships could be cleaned out. The Canadians from the island and two nearby ones returned to their settlements and surrendered their arms taking the oath of neutrality. They did this despite Levis's request they continue fighting, promising them reinforcements in order to compel the British to stay aboard their ships. The Canadians reported that Levis was entrenched with about 4,000 troops about nine miles southward, while Bourlamaque was strengthening his works at Sorel.

The two regiments that made up the Louisbourg division under Lord Andrew Rollo finally joined Murray on the 17th. On his journey upriver, Rollo had landed his 1,300

---

[43] *Ibid.*, 496.

troops at Batiscan, located downriver from Trois-Rivieres and disarmed parishes in that region. Moving past Trois-Rivieres they had taken fire from Canadians and Indians.

More news on the activity of the enemy came in that day as a deserter informed Murray that the French were fortifying the Island of Jesus above Montreal. There was talk of throwing a boom across the river and there was only one vessel, a sloop called *La Marie*, upriver from them. The deserter stated that Levis was south of them watching Murray's advance which was slow due to contrary winds.

Lord Rollo and the troops under his command, along with the rangers, landed their boats a mile below Sorel at 2 a.m. on the 22nd. There they began to burn houses and laid waste to much of the parish. This was something the inhabitants had longed feared from the fleet. Murray had not wanted to do this and in a letter to Pitt explained his actions:

"I found the inhabitants of the parish of Sorel had deserted their habitants, and were in arms; I was therefore under the cruel necessity of burning the greatest part of these poor unhappy people's houses; I pray God this example may suffice, for my nature revolts, when this becomes a necessary part of my duty."[44]

---

[44] *Ibid.*, 504.

After the houses were smoldering ruins, Rollo attempted to draw the French out from behind their entrenchments at Sorel. As they would not budge, Rollo re-embarked and took his force back to the ships. Bourlamaque was surprised his position at Sorel had not been attacked by Rollo knowing he could not put up a serious resistance, as he was low in powder, guns and men as many of the militia had deserted. In hopes of stopping the desertion of the militia, Bourlamaque had some of their houses torched as a warning to the others.

The fleet continued upriver reaching the island of St. Therese, which is located at the east end of the island of Montreal, on the 27th. The rangers and light infantry were landed on the island around 6 p.m.. The rest of the army stayed aboard but were ready to land at the shortest notice with the orders being given the next day for each soldier to have 36 cartridges and three flints.

Good news was brought in by a soldier of the 17th Regiment who had been captured last year and now escaped. He stated that Amherst was at Isle Royale and the bulk of the French army consisting of regulars and chosen Canadians were at Montreal. The Indians had abandoned the French and many of the militia which had been bolstering the regular's ranks had deserted. He was right as this was a serious problem for the French causing the governor to proclaim through the parish that anyone deserting or giving up their arms to the British would face death. Anyone who would not join the army would have their house burned.

On August 31st, half of the light troops (rangers and light infantry) and four companies of grenadiers landed near Varenne where the enemy threw a few shots there way then took off. Once a shore three rockets were set off as a signal for the rest of the light troops to land lower down. Each detachment then marched for the church and center of the parish skirmishing with about 300 enemy troops, 60 of whom where regulars. The church and chapel were easily taken without the loss of a man. That night the grenadiers returned to their ships, while the rangers and light infantry remained at the church. Things were soon to get hot for them the next day.

Around 1 p.m., about 80 Canadians, dividing themselves into small detachments, attacked the rangers at Varenne. It was quickly determined the Canadians were trying to capture a barn near the chapel. The barn was set on fire denying it to the Canadians, but they used the cover of smoke and flames to make an attempt on the chapel. A handful of rangers got there first and beat them back. By this time six light infantrymen, who were expert marksmen, and with some officers moved down from the church and taking up position on the Canadian's flank, opened up on them causing them to fall back. The rangers, covered by a company of light infantry, now took after the Canadians chasing them for almost a mile capturing seven of them. That evening the enemy returned southeast of the church but did not attack. The light infantry torched some buildings which were situated on high ground and commanded their position.

On September 1, the whole parish at Varenne gave up their arms and took the oath of neutrality. More parishes agreed to surrender the next day. The British soon began to entrench at Varenne. Murray now intended to wait for Amherst and Haviland who were not far off.

Chapter 9
Amherst's Advance: August-September, 1760

On August 1, Amherst and Sir William Johnson along with all the chiefs assembled at Oswego boarded the 18 gun snow. At the Indians request, Amherst had agreed to call her the *Onondaga*. A large flag with an Indian head on it was hoisted up as Amherst broke a bottle against the head of the vessel. Then the 80th Regiment of Light Infantry let loose a volley, as did the Royal Highlanders. A gun bellowed from the fort while the newly christened *Onondaga* fired nine of her guns. Johnson then made some speeches and punch was handed out. The chiefs were greatly delighted with the whole ceremony and agreed to go with Amherst on the coming campaign.

In fact a fair number of warriors agreed to go with Amherst. Through the work of Johnson and his Indian officers such as John Butler and Jelles Fonda, they had recruited 706 warriors drawn mostly from the Six Nations, but other tribes as well including 15 Oswegatchies.[45]

They would join the over 10,000 Anglo-American troops who were still assembling. The regulars of Amherst's army consisted of the 1st Battalion and 2nd Battalion of the 42nd Regiment (Royal Highlanders), the 44th, 46th, 55th Regiments, the 4th Battalion of the Royal Americans (the 60th), eight companies of the 77th Regiment, and five companies of the 80th. There were also the two ranger companies. The rest of Amherst's soldiers were provincials made up of a regiment from New Jersey (the New Jersey Blues), three from New York, and four from Connecticut. Colonel George Williamson commanded a detachment of 157 men from the Royal Artillery.

The grenadiers from each regiment, as was often the case, were embodied into one corps numbering almost 600 men under the command of Lieutenant-Colonel Massey. The light infantry were also incorporated into one corps also numbering about 600 men and put under the command of Lieutenant-Colonel William Amherst, the commander's younger brother.

While the bulk of the troops were to travel in bateaux, Lieutenant-Colonel Amherst's light infantry, the 80th, and the rangers were issued 86 whaleboats. Bateaux were to be used by these light troops to carry their baggage. Each bateaux was to have eight oars, six paddles and four setting poles and were to carry about 20 men or so, plus provisions not exceeding 14 barrels of flour or 12 of pork.

---

[45] Actually 1,330 men, women and children, mostly Six Nations, had assembled at Oswego by August 5, but as stated only 703 joined the expedition

The whaleboats each had eight oars, 12 paddles and only two setting poles and were to carry 14 men. Each corps was to mark their bateaux on the starboard bow and organized into two ranks, while the colonels in command of the brigades would be allowed the faster moving whaleboats.

Colonel Frederick Haldimand took command of a detachment consisting of Massey's grenadiers, Amherst's Light Infantry, the 1st Battalion of the 42nd, and the rangers who moved out of Oswego on August 7th. They were to assist Loring and his two vessels the *Onondaga* and the other snow named the *Mohawk* in finding a channel down the St. Lawrence River to Fort Levis. On each of the snows were placed 30 men with an officer, while two engineers with a bateau laden with axes and entrenching tools set off with them.[46]

Journeying north along the eastern shore of Lake Ontario, Haldimand's corps was hammered by a high wind. Some of the bateaux proved themselves to be poorly built and were staved in spilling their contents in the lake. A whaleboat was lost too. In all Haldimand lost a good deal of pork and flour along with some firearms and 9,000 cartridges were spoiled. Things were not off to a good start.

Preparation continued at Oswego on the 9th for the main body of the army to depart the next day as the bateaux were loaded with provisions. Almost sixty

---

[46] The *Onondaga* had a crew of 100 men , while the *Mohawk* had 90 men. These 30 men would likely be in addition to the crews.

artificers were left to continue work on the interior of Fort Ontario. Also staying behind were 290 sick men and 169 soldiers for garrison duty. More grimly a general court martial was held in which ten men were condemned to death. Four were executed that evening, while one managed to escape.

At first light the drums began to roll on the morning of the 10th as the troops prepared to depart. Their tents were struck and camp equipment loaded. Then the regiments headed to their assigned bateaux and the army began to embark. Amherst set out with the regulars and artillery, with the brown coated 80th leading the way at 10 a.m.. This part of the armada numbered over 5,500 men. Gage was left to command the provincials numbering almost 4,500 men, who were to bring up the rear. He set of at noon. In all the army had over 650 bateaux, as well five specially built armed row galleys. Extras bateaux were brought along to replace those lost by Haldimand.

The wind began to pick up in the evening forcing Amherst to have his army row into a creek about 30 miles from Oswego[47]. The troops at the front of the armada made land about sunset while the rear didn't make shore to near midnight. Some of bateaux were staved in during the night landing and deemed unfit for service. An artillery bateaux was sunk as was one belonging to the 77th. Fortunately nobody drowned, which could not be said for a soldier of the 80th who fell overboard. Gage with

---

[47] The tributary was called Riviere de Sable by the French. Probably Sandy Creek.

some of the provincials, meanwhile, returned back to Oswego because of the wind.

The wind continued to blow hard the next day keeping Amherst some venturing out with his armada until about 2 p.m. when the weather began to improve. Amherst made about 8 mile before stopping for the night.

That same day, Gage set off again from Oswego with the element of his provincials that had turned back the day before. They made the 30 mile or so journey to the creek Amherst had just departed from. Gage then pushed on in his whaleboat and caught up with Amherst who ordered him to bring the provincials on if they weren't too played out. Otherwise they were to push on in the morning.

Also battling the wind at Oswego was Captains Jelles Fonda and John Butler. While Johnson had set off with about half the Indians with Amherst on the 10th, Fonda and Butler attempted to leave on the 11th in the morning after they waited for the warriors to sober up, but were back by noon because of the wind. They tried again that night and had better success. The next day they caught up with Johnson.

The journey so far had been unpleasant for Amherst's flotilla as rough weather had smashed boats, destroyed provisions, spoiled cartridges and made some men sea sick. Sleeping arrangements were less than ideal as many of the troops were forced to sleep in the bateaux, there not being enough cleared ground for the men to camp. On August 12 though, the weather was improving and the army set off for Mouse Bay where there would be more elbow room for the soldiers.

On the 13th, Amherst set off about 9 a.m. in three columns. The regulars were on the right, the Connecticut and New Jersey troops in the center, with the New York provincials and artillery on the left. The troops had a beautiful day in which they rowed about 30 miles before making camp at what Amherst called Robertson's Bay. The last of the troops rowed in about 10 p.m.. Fort Levis now lay only a few days away.

From his Indian scouts and two vessels Pouchot was aware of the British built up at Oswego. He also learned on July 22 that British allied Indian scouts had been reconnoitering around La Presentation from an Indian woman who said they asked a number of questions such as how many troops were at Fort Levis. The woman had told the Indian scouts that she and the other women were planning to go to Montreal as they were afraid of the coming army. The scouts told her she and the others would not be harmed and that they should separate themselves from the French. Despite this claim, five days later 67 women, children and the elderly left for Montreal.

More bad news was brought to Pouchot's attention when he learned that the *Iroquoise* had been damaged in the middle of the St. Lawrence River by hitting some rocks above Point-au-Baril on August 1. Pouchot quickly sent some bateaux to aid her. Four days later the two vessels were anchored at La Presentation. The *Iroquoise's* damage was serious enough with fifteen feet of her keel broken.

The vessel remained out of service under the protection of the fort's guns.[48]

On the 8th, an Oswegatchie chief arrived from Oswego with two deputies, an Oneida and a Mohawk, sent by the Six Nations to engage the Oswegatchies to stay neutral. The chief then told Pouchot that Amherst had 10,000 or 15,000 men and described the uniforms of the various regiments.

Two days later Pouchot was at Isle Piquet to take part in a council with the Iroquois's deputies. The deputies urged not only the Oswegatchies, but the Kahnawakes and Kanesetakes as well, to remain neutral and to let the whites do the fighting. They added that Johnson would receive them well. Pouchot attempted to counter their arguments warning that once the French were gone the English would treat them poorly. Despite Pouchot's words, the Oswegatchies and other Canadian Iroquois agreed to be neutral. The French commander with about 300 men would have no Indian help in facing the massive Anglo-American army only days away.

Further up the St. Lawrence River, Amherst's armada set out at 10 a.m. on August 14 in three columns this time with the artillery on the right, the provincials in the center, and the regulars on the left. They rowed about 15 miles

---

[48] What happened to the *Iroquoise* is somewhat of a mystery. On August 13 Amherst recorded in his journal that the guns were being taken out of the vessel and put on Isle Royale. However, Pouchot in his memoirs would state that the vessel was repaired on August 15. As the vessel was not to play a role in the upcoming fighting it would seem the *Iroquoise* remained out of service.

through the scenic Thousand Islands before stopping for a rainy night on Haldimand Island and some of the nearby islands as well. Travelling through the numerous islands was very different then what the charts showed. Fortunately Amherst had sent a couple of officers ahead "to view the properest Route" which was a great aid to the armada.[49]

After the regulars had received their provisions for four days, the army set off around 9 a.m. the next day again in three columns with the regulars on the right, the artillery in the center, and the provincials on the left. The weather had cleared making for a fine day as the armada continued through the Thousands Island region of the St. Lawrence River.

Along the way they met Loring with the *Onondaga* and *Mohawk* at anchor having trouble finding a channel through the islands. Amherst pushed on for about 20 miles reaching the advance post Haldimand had established with his corps at around 5 p.m. The provincials were ordered to prepare four days of provisions and see to their arms. To help Loring, two Oswegatchies were spent back to pilot the vessels downriver. From the Oswegatchies, Amherst learned of the damaged French vessel and decided not to wait for Loring to engage the remaining French vessel.

Amherst ordered a howitzer to be placed in one of the row galleys that was intended to mount a 12-pounder. As

---

[49] Jeffery Amherst, *The Journal of Jeffery Amherst,* (Toronto: The Ryerson Press, 1933) p. 230.

the carriage for the 12-pounder was not completed before the army departed, it was converted to hold a howitzer. The other four galleys all boasted 12-pounders. A soldier from the 80th and an artillery officer, meanwhile, were sent back upriver to get some supplies from Loring.

The armada set out again on the morning of the 16th in three columns. The advance guard now consisted not only of the 80th, but also the rangers, and both the light infantry and grenadiers corps. They were now under the command of Colonel Francis Grant. As the boats moved downriver, the carpenters worked on finishing the howitzer's carriage on the galley along the way. The advance guard's baggage bateaux were sent back to travel with the artillery's column of boats. Amherst, who was travelling with the advance guard, hoped to have his army make Oswegatchie this day. With no wind, however, and it getting late Amherst sent back orders to Gage to have the bulk of the army encamp at Pointe-au-Baril.

Amherst pushed on with the advance guard who had spotted the *Outaouaise* near Oswegatchie. Darkness over took the advance guard before they could engage the vessel. Amherst ordered the advance guard to head for Oswegatchie to encamp.

Two signal guns boomed from the *Outaouaise* when the advance guard was spotted. Three more guns blasted warnings later on when the advance guard's campfires were spotted along the south shore of the river. In the end the advance guard had not encamped at Oswegatchie as Johnson had desired them not to enter the Indian town at night as it would cause a panic among the people.

The *Outaouaise* attempted to move up river the next morning to attack the unprotected British bateaux. The wind calmed and with the current against him, Captain Pierre Boucher de Labroquerie was not to get far with his vessel before he was attacked by the five row galleys under the command of Colonel Williamson. Cannon fire echoed across the St. Lawrence River for over two hours as the *Outaouaise* battled the five British galleys. These smaller vessels pounded 118 shots at the *Outaouaise* who returned 72 before Labroquerie struck the vessel's colors. When the gun smoke finally cleared the French vessel had three dead and 12 wounded. Williamson had one killed and two wounded. The captured ship with its 18-pounder, seven 12-pounders two 8-poundrs and four swivel guns was now in British hands and renamed the *Williamson*. Pouchot had dispatched four boats armed with swivels to help the *Outaouaise*, but she surrendered before they arrived.

Carpenters set to work to repair the galleys and the captured vessel damaged in the engagement. The 100 French prisoners were taken ashore and replaced with Amherst's men. The army, meanwhile, arrived at Oswegatchie which caused a panic among the Indian inhabitants causing some to flee into the surrounding forest. Those that stayed received the British regulars and American provincials kindly. Eventually the others would return and a cordial relationship was established.

Amherst dispatched two detachments of 120 men

under the command of Captain Adam Williamson and Lieutenant Ratser, both engineers, to head down river on both sides of the St. Lawrence and scout out the French fort.[50] Expecting his scouting parties back anytime soon, Amherst had the advance guard strike their tents at 3 a.m. and be ready to move despite the pounding rain. Ratser did not return until 8 a.m., while Williamson made his appearance two hours later. Both engineers reported to Amherst the lay of the land by Fort Levis.

Amherst decided he would pass the fort along both the north and south shore. The 80th would act as the advance guard for the division cruising along the north shore. The 80th were to travel in two boats abreast, followed by the three row galleys. Following them would be the 1st Brigade consisting of the light infantry and grenadiers; the 2nd Battalion of the 42nd Highlanders; the 46th and 77th; followed by a portion of the artillery and the New Jersey Blues; as well as a good portion of the Indians with Johnson. Amherst himself would accompany this division.

The troops passing along the south shore consisted of the two rangers companies leading the way, with two row galleys protecting the bateaux. Next came the 2nd Brigade which was made up of the 55th, 4th Battalion of the Royal Americans, the 44th, and Colonel Phineas Lyman's 1st Connecticut Regiment bringing up the rear. They were under the command of Colonel Haldimand. The

---

[50] These detachments were accompanied by Indian Department officers Captain Fonda and Captain John Lotteridge along with some warriors.

Williamson, meanwhile, was to sail to the center of the river and engage the fort. The rest of the army and heavy artillery remained at Oswegatchie with Gage.

The division moving along the north shore came under fire from Fort Levis as they passed by. Thinking the British intended to make a landing on the island, Pouchot positioned nine of his cannons to fire up river.

The 80th and the galleys came under fire by the four guns Pouchot had trained on them. In the brisk cannon fire one row galley was sunk, while two men were killed in another galley. Next came the whaleboats and bateaux enduring the fire having seven men wounded and one unfortunate soldier having his thigh shot off. The boats and oars also took a number of hits. The 80th captured the two islands below the fort, while the armed row galleys swung around and anchored off one of these islands to help protect the oncoming troops. The 80th were on alert to be ready to quickly board their whaleboats and defend their fellow soldiers should the French send out armed bateaux.

Amherst, meanwhile, ordered the other regiments to land on the north shore out of sight of the enemy guns. To lessen the casualties in passing Fort Levis, Amherst had the bateaux spread out reducing their chances of being hit. The French would fire 150 shots off at the passing enemy troops. Pouchot knew many of the British officers passing by and bade some of them a good day.

It would be between 10 and 11 p.m. before the last bateaux rowed past the French fort and encamped for the night. Actually the next day it was discovered that not all the New Jersey troops had set off yet.

On the two abandoned islands, Isle Galot and Ile Picquet, captured by the 80th a number of scalps were discovered. Also found were barrels of pitch, a great quantity of iron, a couple of swivels guns, shot and tools. On Ile Piquet some homes and a chapel were torched by the pro-British Indians which they took to be Frenchman's homes. After finding scalps in some huts, they were set on fire as well.

While the *Williamson* traded shots with the fort, Haldimand's division passed along the south shore headed for a point of land that would allow the batteries to be within 700 or 800 yards of the fort. They did not have the trouble Amherst did.

On the 19th, Amherst with Williamson and Lieutenant-Colonel William Eyre reconnoitered the two nearby islands, La Cuisse and La Magdelaine, about 500 yards from the fort where it was determined to erect batteries. It was decided that the island batteries would consist of three 24-pounders, three 12-pounders, and a ten inch mortar. It turned out one of the 12-pounders was back at Oswego so something would have to replace it. Two 12-pounders would be placed in the battery on the point of land on the south shore of the river. Two construct these batteries 500 men in their waistcoats were rowed by light bateaux out to the two islands to begin breaking ground and cutting and making fascines which were large bundles of sticks used in supporting earthworks and filling ditches.

Amherst sent orders to Oswegatchie for the three New York provincial regiments and the heavy artillery to move down from the village at night. Haldimand on the south shore was ordered to begin constructing a battery there.

The *Williamson* and Fort Levis trade shots for part of the morning stopping around 10 a.m.. In the evening the *Williamson* was joined by the *Onondaga* and the *Mohawk*. All three vessels were ordered to anchor at random shot[51] from Fort Levis, but to avoid returning fire if fired on. Meanwhile, nineteen men of the captured French brig's crew were put to work as river pilots with one going to each corps and one being put aboard the *Williamson*.

On the 20th, Amherst went and viewed eight different islands between Isle Galot and Ile Picquet. Woodhull, commander of the 3rd New York Provincials, wrote that some of islands which were deserted at first sight of Amherst's army, had buildings on them and had an abundance of corn, beans, squash, and cabbage along with some hogs and fowls. The rest of the army, except one Connecticut regiment, were ordered down from Oswegatchie. Work progressed on the batteries, occasionally fired on by the French. Pouchot having only 5,000 pounds of powder at the beginning of the siege had to use it conservatively.

Work on the batteries continued throughout the next day with three reliefs. The French still continued to fire on

---

[51] In naval terms the greatest distance a ball can be fired from an artillery piece that has its breech resting on the bed of its carriage.

the laborers, being careful to preserve their powder. They managed to kill five men, three with one shot. More men were killed on the 22nd due to French artillery fire. All the men that could be spared were busy working on the batteries and entrenchment. The guns were drawn up, but it would not be until the next day that they would open on Pouchot's little garrison.

Early in the morning on the 23rd, Colonel Williamson sought permission from Amherst to fire on the French with the batteries that were ready. This amounted to the batteries on the point of land on the south shore and some of the batteries on the islands that were completed. Work would continue on the batteries that weren't.

Amherst gave the go ahead, and the guns opened up at around 7 a.m.. A French artillery officer was standing by Pouchot pointing out the caliber of the British guns when he was killed by a cannon ball that smashed through his loins. Not long afterwards Pouchot was hit in the back by a ten foot long piece of wood sent flying by a 12 inch bomb. Although badly bruised, Pouchot continued to stay in the action.

After a few hours of pounding away at Fort Levis it was decided to storm the fort. The grenadiers were assigned the task and supported by the three vessels which moved in closer to the fort. Leaving their coats behind, the grenadiers were ordered to wear their waistcoats and forage caps and be armed with only swords, tomahawks and axes. Officers and sergeants were the only ones with muskets. Marksmen were placed on each of the ship's tops with the intentions of making things hot for the French gunners. Also aiding the grenadiers were two armed galleys and 300 men from the light infantry corps and the 80th.

With the men ready to go, Amherst ordered Loring to take his vessels in. About 1:15 p.m., according to Loring his vessel, the *Onondaga,* anchored within about 25 yards of the fort, while the other two vessels were a little closer. For three quarters of an hour the *Mohawk* lay by Fort Levis firing on it, but taking a pounding from the French guns in return. Pouchot positioned 154 men and officers to meet the grenadiers should they attempt to storm the fort. The attack never came.

To avoid being sunk the battered *Mohawk* headed down river. The *Williamson* joined her half an hour later when her cable was cut by a French shot and was forced down river. She too had taken a pounding from the fort and had three feet of water in her hold. With these two ships down river, Amherst decided to call off any attack against Fort Levis.

The *Onondaga* had remained on station and shot it out with the fort until about 3:30 p.m.. With most of her ammunition spent, eight guns dismounted, and everything tore to piece, Loring sent a boat to shore to find out when the grenadiers and light infantry were going to attack. He was informed the attack was canceled. Then according to Loring, he asked for boats to help tow the *Onondaga,* but none could be obtained. Loring now thought it high time to save the *Onondaga* and attempted to limp away with his battered vessel, but the strong current caused her to ground near the fort.

Pouchot's guns increased their fire hammering away at the ship. After getting the sails down, Loring ordered his crew into the hold to protect them from the storm of lead. Pouchot had ordered the blacksmith to cut old irons which were put in sacks and push down the bore of the guns in which was added a cannon ball. It played havoc on the British. The *Onondaga's* crew hoped help would come, but when it didn't by 5:30 p.m., the men, according to Loring, could not understand while they were being sacrificed and insisted the ship strike her colours. Loring refused.

With two more men hit and the ship on fire in two places from the enemy's red hot shot, the crew went up on the deck and struck the colours. Loring attempted to persuade the men to stand by the vessel. They refused insisting on going ashore. Some of them climbed into a small boat planning to do just that. Loring snatched up a musket and said he would shoot the first man to lay "his Hand on an Oar".[52] His threat got the men to go back on board the battered *Onondaga*. Loring then ordered his second-in-command, Joshua Thorton, and a couple of men to row ashore to Fort Levis. Loring claimed he sent them to the French to buy time in allowing him to get assistance from the grenadiers and light infantry 600 yards away behind an island.

The French, meanwhile, were calling out to him to come ashore, which Loring refused. Pouchot mentions in

---

[52]Knox, *Journal*, 551

his memoirs Thornton coming ashore stating he had come to surrender and was held as a hostage.

A British battery seeing the boat, which they supposed had either Loring or Thorton aboard, head for the French fort fired on it. No damage was done, but when the boat was spotted rowing back, Captain Williamson, an engineer at one of the batteries, fired a gun on her believing the French were attempting to take possession of the ship. The boat headed back to shore with a seriously wounded man.

Grenadiers under the command of Lieutenant Pennington in two galleys were ordered to board the *Onondaga* and hoist her colours back up. Loring, meanwhile, had his right calf ripped off by a cannon ball. The grenadiers climbing aboard the ship quickly cleared the deck after losing about a third of their men killed or wounded to the French fire. They sought cover in the hold to escape the murderous storm of lead. Empty bateaux were also sent to get the artillery stores of the vessel, but the French heavy fire made this impossible. The wounded were evacuated about 8 p.m. Six hours later the rest of men were taken ashore. The ship by this time was almost full of water.

The first attempt on Fort Levis had not gone well. The *Onondaga* was out of action while the *Mohawk* and the *Williamson* were both shot up pretty bad. In fact Amherst ordered two 12-pounders from the latter ship to be sent to Haldimand's battery on the south shore. Pouchot, on the other hand, did not have things all his own way as he lost 40 men killed or wounded from his small garrison.

The batteries continued to pound away on Fort Levis on the 24th. Both the *Williamson* and the *Mohawk* were being repaired. Amherst ordered two whaleboats with a detachment of light infantry out to the *Onondaga* that night to guard her. On board the light infantry men found two New Yorkers who probably had been left behind drunk when the vessel's crew had left earlier. One of the men was wounded.

During the day, Amherst had ordered his batteries to decrease their fire a little, only to increase them at night to prevent the French from repairing their battered fort which took quite a pounding that day. Fires had caught in the ruins of the fort's magazine as well at the commandant's quarters. Fortunately for the French these fires were put out.

The British batteries continued their pounding of Fort Levis on the 25th. Pouchot fought back with his few remaining guns, but he could do little against the British batteries which had increased their fire and were lobbing red hot shot and fire-pots at the splintered French fort.

With the ramparts ruined and fires breaking out, Pouchot, with the advice of his officers, had a parley beat and sought surrender terms. The guns fell silent while Amherst sent back his terms stating the garrison would become prisoners of war or hostilities would soon recommence.[53] With only two guns still able to fire and no

---

[53] Amherst stated that British deserters and Indians were not included in the surrender terms.

more cannon balls and his fort in ruins, Pouchot had little choice. He surrendered. Colonel Massey and three companies of grenadiers were quickly sent to take possession of the fort.

Amherst heard that the Indians were still angry over finding Mohawk scalps in the deserted cabins and intended to enter the fort and massacre the garrison. He quickly ordered Johnson to intervene, who managed to persuade them to return to their camp. With the crisis averted Johnson informed Amherst that he thought many of the Indians would leave. The commander-in-chief thought the army was capable of continuing on without them, although he wished to preserve their friendship. Amherst warned that if they committed any acts of cruelty on their way home he would chastise them.

The situation did not improve when a British or possibly a provincial officer was overheard mentioning that the English after the campaign would return and exterminate the Indian race. In the coming days over 500 Indians would return home, leaving 185 who stayed with Amherst's army.

Although the Indians may not have entered the ruins of Fort Levis in mass,[54] a sutler and two spruce brewers did and took 11 French firelocks and some goods. They were caught and had 300 lashes across their backs which were bloody raw messes of meat when the whipping mercifully stopped. Strict orders were also given that the sutlers

---

[54] A few Natives climbed in over the walls. Johnson would later write the Indians were angry over seeing the grenadiers loot the fort and not being allowed to join in went home angry.

were not to barter or purchase arms, ammunition or clothing from the Indians. Severe punishment would fall on any who did. A sutler was caught on the 30th selling rum to an Indian and was sentenced to 300 lashes.

The siege of Fort Levis and the naval action on the 18th had cost Amherst 21 men killed and 23 wounded. The French had 13 killed, 35 wounded and 291 captured. From the garrison 36 Canadians were taken to act as pilots for the journey down river through the rapids to Montreal. The rest of the garrison was sent onto Oswego under escort for their journey to New York as prisoners of war. Thorton was no longer a prisoner of Pouchot, but instead was arrested by the Provost Guard and held for three days before being released and sent home. Work began on repairing the fort, which was renamed Fort William Augustus. The French vessel *Iroquoise* was raised while the other vessels were repaired.

On the 28th, Johnson had good news for Amherst when he learned from three Indians that Murray's ships had reached Montreal. The next day Captain Jacob Naunauphtaunk arrived with some French Indians. He had been captured with Kennedy by the Abenakis back in the fall of 1759 while under the pretense of a flag of truce. He had been held on a French prison ship until his release was secured by a priest. Amherst recorded in his journal that Jacob "brought me a letter from a Priest to offer Peace on the Indians side."[55] The priest was Pierre Roubaud, a missionary at St. Francis, but now apparently living at

---

[55] Amherst, *Journal*, 241.

Akwesasne. Amherst sent Jacob off as peace envoy to St. Francis. Like many of the other tribes once allied to the French, they now sought peace with the British to preserve their own future.

Even before the army left Oswego, Johnson had sent Indian messengers to the tribes residing near Montreal offering them peace and protection. During the siege of Fort Levis, Johnson had met with deputies from the Seven Nations ratifying a treaty with them where they agreed to remain neutral as long as the English treated them as friends. Ten Akwesasnes even joined Amherst's army.

Around noon on August 31, Amherst resumed his campaign down the St. Lawrence River. Two hundred men were left behind at Fort William Augustus, while another 215 men who were sick were left at a make shift hospital at Oswegatchie. Leading Amherst's armada were the rangers and the 80th along with Johnson's remaining Indians.

The first rapids they encountered were the Galops rapids and they were not severe. The army made 24 miles before stopping for the night. The next day the army passed through Rapid de Plat, which also was not very severe, but things changed when they reached the Long Sault Rapids. Here the roaring rapids stretched for nine miles. To prevent ambush from Chevalier de la Corne and his men, the rangers disembarked from their whaleboats and scouted the forest on both side of the rapids.

With the rapids safe from ambush, Amherst and the advance guard shot through them. Amherst had ordered in the morning that at the Long Sault Rapids or long Fall as he called them, the boats where to go through single file. The men were warned not to panic at the appearance of the rapids as the commander-in-chief stated there "is no danger in the rapids".[56]

Although Amherst's whale boat took on water a few times, everybody made it through safely. While camp was set out at Point Maline[57] for the night, scouts were sent ahead to view the shores on both side of river up ahead. None of the enemy were discovered. That same day, September 1, Sir William had gone onto Akwesasne to assure them no harm would come to them.

On September 2, Gage's and most of the main body of the army caught up with Amherst and the advance guard. The 1st Battalion of the 42nd Highlanders had bad luck when shooting the Long Sault Rapids as they kept too close to the shore and had one boat staved in drowning four men. Although the last division had yet to arrive, Amherst ordered the rest of army to set off rowing in four columns entering the waters of Lake St. Francis and pushing on 24 miles or so to Point Beaudette.[58]

During the night it rained hard with a fierce wind which continued into the morning preventing Amherst from setting out. Instead Indian scouts were sent out to

[56] William Hervey, *Journals of the Hon. William Hervey in North America and Europe From 1755-1814*, (St. Edmund's: Paul & Mathew, Butter Market, 1906) p. 120.
[57] Near modern Cornwall, Ontario.
[58] Near where the Beaudette River empties into the St. Lawrence River.

the Cedars, a settlement along the St. Lawrence River, where they took a prisoner and returned. From the prisoner it was learned that La Corne with 400 men had been at the Cedars, but had withdrawn to Montreal when his advanced guard had seen Amherst's bateaux.

On September 4, the army set off again about 6 a.m.. As they were nearing the Canadian settlements the order was given that nothing was to be plundered from them or those who did would face being executed. Three hours after setting off they had passed through Lake St. Francis and soon were to encounter the Coteau rapids, Cedar rapids and the Cascades. The first one was not bad, but the others were to cost the army dearly in men and boats.

At the Cedars, the bulk of the army was put ashore to make the boats lighter and the men marched to the end of the Cascades. Despite the fact that every corps had a river pilot and these pilots were sent back to help guide other boats through the rushing, roaring dangerous waters, 37 bateaux were lost, along with 17 whaleboats and a galley. Some artillery stores were lost and some guns, which were hoped to be recovered, and more seriously 84 men perished, many from the 42nd Highlanders and provincials, in shooting the rapids.

Lieutenant John Grant, an officer in the 2nd Battalion of the 42nd, recalled when he passed through the Cedar Rapids his boat was whirled about and filled with water. He saw several bateaux upset with soldiers struggling in the rapids crying for help.

Only part of the army got through the Cascades

before it got too late in the day. The rangers, the 80th, the grenadiers and light infantry, along with the 1st and 2nd Brigade of regulars encamped for the night on the Isle Perrot about 3 miles from the Cascades. The inhabitants had fled at the sight of the army, but slowly trickled back and surrendered.

Passage of Amherst's Army down the rapids of the St. Lawrence by Thomas Davies (Library and Archives Canada).

The provincials and part of the artillery, meanwhile, encamped for the night at the Cedars. The following day they joined the rest of the army at Isle Perrot where the boats were being repaired. The inhabitants, meanwhile, came in and took the oath of allegiance to the British.

Montreal lay only a day away. The Anglo-American armies were converging. To the south Haviland's army was not far away. The fall of New France was imminent.

Chapter 10
Haviland's Advance: August-September, 1760

On August 11, Haviland's army of 3,400 men set out from Crown Point. By noon the vessels were heading north in three columns. Acting as the advance guard for the armada was Major Rogers and 600 rangers along with his Indian company of 70 men rowing about half a mile ahead of the main body. Following the rangers were the light infantry and grenadiers drawn from the 17th and 27th Regiments under Lieutenant-Colonel John Darby. Both the right and left wing of the armada were made up provincials from Massachusetts, Rhode Island and New Hampshire. The British regulars made up of the 17th and 27th Regiments, along with four companies of the Royals were positioned in the center. Behind them came the artillery and the sutlers.

At sunset after having made six miles the armada landed on the west side of Lake Champlain for the night.

Captain Jenks of Massachusetts spent an uncomfortable night sleeping on barrels in the bateaux. He was up early the next morning and with the rest of the army set out a sunrise rowing down the lake for three or four miles. Then the breeze turned to a strong wind from the north making travelling difficult, especially for the sailing vessels. The armada stopped along the east bank of the lake for the night.

At 8 a.m. on the 13th, the armada set off again only to have the wind spring up again four hours later. The armada continued onto about 4 p.m. when they encamped on the west side of the lake. They had come about 28 miles from Crown Point.

The next morning the army set off a sunrise with sails spread out. About 11 a.m., a heavy gale hit them hard causing everybody to shift for themselves. Battling the rough waters and hard wind the boats made for the north side of Schuylers Island. Ten rangers were drowned when their boats split.

The weather was not as severe on the 15th as the army set out again at sunrise. The enemy was close by as Jenks ominously expected "to be amongst bad neighbours before night."[59] He wasn't far off. The 16th found the army setting off at dawn. The armada rowed across a large bay and formed up in line with two boats abreast, the whole stretching back about four miles. At the mouth of the Richelieu River the French vessels appeared but were

---

[59] Samuel Jenks, *Diary of Captain Samuel Jenks during the French and Indian War 1760*, (Cambridge: John Wilson and Son, 1890, reprinted from Proceedings of the Massachusetts Historical Society, 1890), 19.

quickly driven off. Jenks and the rest of the army's boats were formed up about a mile and half from Isle-aux-Noix preparing to land on the east shore of the river. As soon as the signal was given, the troops began to row and landed without any trouble from the French.

The ships, meanwhile, fired on the fort and French vessels covering the landing of the troops. Rogers and Darby quickly led their men through the wet terrain for the ground opposite the fort on the east side. They took it with no opposition. Jenks and the other provincials also struggled with wet terrain making breastworks. These works were manned all night in case the French tried anything.

Over the next few days the troops were busy constructing batteries. Jenks and his men were busy constructing more breastworks on the 19th while enduring fire from the French fort that lay only half a cannon shot away. Luckily for Jenks and his men no one was harmed.

As the French continued to fire away, work continued on the batteries by 800 provincials. Jenks had over 150 men carrying timber for the batteries. On the 21st ten men were wounded from the enemy fire. Jenks, himself, had several close calls. Worn from a hard day work, Jenks just crawled into his bed for sleep that night when all the troops were ordered to arms. A large party of the enemy had been discovered pushing off from Isle-aux-Noix in their boats towards the British and American camp. The fires were quickly put out and the troops manned the breastworks waiting to receive the enemy. Nothing happened as the French turned back when they found out they were spotted. While pickets were kept out, the troops were ordered back to their tents. This was not the end.

Nerves must have been jittery for about an hour before dawn a sentry thought he spotted the enemy and fired his musket, which caused three or four more sentries to fire as well. The army was quickly on their feet and manning the breastworks waiting for the enemy yet again. Causing more alarm the captain of the picket thought he saw a man outside the lines and challenged him three times. No answer. Somebody gave the order to fire and the whole of the battalion Jenks belonged to let loose a volley, which spread down the line as it was impossible to get the men to cease firing even though there was nobody to shoot at. Finally the mistake was realized and the troops returned to their tents.

By the 22nd, the regulars and provincials camp was looking good. All the trees had been cleared out so no one could get hurt by falling limbs caused by French cannon fire. They had a fine breastwork that was both in front and in the rear of the camp. The troops still bustled with work setting up the siege. Jenks and his men helped clear a road through the camp to allow the guns to be drawn up below the enemy's fort to a point of land where a battery was to be erected which would cut communication to Fort St. Jean. Mortars and cannons were being unloaded and it was hoped that three batteries would be completed by night fall.

The beating of drums sounded out from the British and American works on the afternoon of the 23rd. When they stopped the bands took over playing music. Then finally the provincials finished the musical interlude with the singing of psalms. When they were done, the British guns opened around 3 p.m. and began pounding the French fort. The night was alive with gunfire as men attempting to cut away the tree barricade across the river were annoyed by enemy musket fire. British guns blasted grape fire at the French troops in return.

Darby proposed to Haviland a daring mission to take the enemy's vessels consisting of two tartans,[60] a schooner and radeau (barge) anchored near Isle-aux-Noix. After getting the go ahead, Darby led a force of two companies of regulars along with Rogers and four ranger companies and Captain Solomon's Indian company through the woods dragging two howitzers and a 6-pounder with them. Once they were opposite the French vessels they pushed the guns out of the forest and opened a brisk fire on the enemy on the morning of the 25th.

The French were caught by surprise and a lucky first shot from the 6-pounder cut the cable of the radeau causing the boat to drift to the east shore where the rangers and regulars were. The other vessels attempted to escape down river towards Fort St. Jean. They had made about two miles downriver when they went aground.

Darby quickly ordered Rogers to go after the vessels. Rogers and his rangers crossed the river and soon got

---

[60] A tartan or tartane is a small ship.

opposite the grounded vessels which were located off shore. While some rangers laid down a covering fire on the vessels, other stripped down and plunged in the river swimming towards one of the vessels armed with tomahawks. The French crew surrendered as the tomahawk wielding rangers climbed aboard.

Darby, meanwhile, boarded the radeau and sailed her downriver capturing the other two vessels. After Haviland was informed of the daring action, he sent down men to man the vessels. The French now had no vessels left other than some row galleys and bateaux.

Inside the French fort, the troops endured the British pounding which had their works sighted in everywhere. Fortunately for them the ground was sandy which helped reduce the casualties. Adding to the French's misery was the fact that provisions were running low. The French commander, Bougainville, was now faced with a dilemma. A French regular officer with a handful of Indian guides arrived on the 27th around 10 a.m. carrying with him two letters - one from the governor, and the other from his commanding officer, Levis.

Governor Vaudreuil's letter gave Bougainville permission to surrender the fort or retire if possible, while Levis told him to hold on to the last extremity. The post commander showed one of his officers, the Scottish Jacobite Chevalier Johnstone, the letters and asked his advice.

Johnstone pointed out that hunger would force them to surrender in a couple of days if they stayed, while the garrison would be of great importance in the defense of Montreal. During the summer Isle-aux-Noix defenders had been re-enforced giving them about 1,450 men. Finally the Jacobite stated that Vaudreuil was in overall command not Levis and escape was still possible through the north side of the island where 300 paces of swampy ground had prevented the British from establishing a post no closer than half a mile away. Bougainville decided the garrison would retreat.

It was decided the fort would be evacuated at 10 p.m. which was none too soon for the Indian guides who were impatient to get away from the British shelling. Bougainville ordered all the boats to be mended and ready at a moment's notice. He took the caution to have all boats, canoes and dugouts moved away from the riverside to prevent any desertion which might jeopardize the evacuation.

Compagnies Franches de la Marine officer M. le Borgne was ordered to remain on the island with 40 men to keep up a smart fire from the battery of seven or eight cannons as long as the ammunition lasted. This would hopefully cover the French retreat across the river.

With everything in place, Bougainville's troops silently made their way down to the water's edge around 10 p.m., while their cannons boomed away. Small boats for two hours rowed back and forth across the river ferrying the troops to the mainland. All this was done without catching the British's attention.

While the guns continued to boom from the fort to

about 1 a.m., Bougainville's troops set out at a half run cutting through the forest. For twelve hours they pushed on, sometimes through swampy ground where men were sinking to their waists in spots. To their dismay, Johnstone would later write, they discovered that all their exertion had not got them very far as their guide had got them off course causing them to get turned around and they were now only about a mile and half from Isle-aux-Noix.

They now took the road that led to Fort St. Jean. Johnstone by this time was worn out and could barely lift his legs. The thoughts of falling into the hands of the enemy's Indians gave him the extra push he needed to continue on. By 4 p.m. the French troops staggered into a settlement about a four or five miles from Fort St. Jean having lost about 80 men in the rugged journey. Here Bougainville gave them a much needed rest. Johnstone managed to draw up enough strength to get in a boat heading down river for St. Jean.

Meanwhile back at Isle-aux-Noix , the fort was now in British hands as Borgne had surrendered. The heavy artillery fire to cover the French retreat had not deceived everyone as Jenks commented that "this we take as their last words."[36]

On the morning of the 28th, Darby's grenadiers and light infantry took possession of the fort. That same day, Jenks in command of 100 men was busy drawing the guns out of the batteries and taking them to the wharf to load

[36]Jenks, *Diary*, 23.

them on vessels. The tree barricades were finally cut away opening up the Richelieu River for the British vessels.

It was not until the 29th that Haviland ordered Rogers to follow after Bougainville and to go no further than St. Jean twenty miles away. With his whole command of six ranger companies and the Indian company, Rogers set out in bateaux. At day light on the 30th Rogers and his rangers arrived at St. Jean only to find it consumed in flames. Two prisoners were picked up which revealed that Bougainville had continued his retreat towards Montreal.

Rogers ordered the log houses near the river to be repaired and left 200 rangers to guard the boats. Then he quickly set off with the remaining 400 rangers and the Indians about 8 a.m. in pursuit. He overtook the French rearguard of about 200 men and forced them back onto the main body. Bougainville did not make a stand as Rogers hoped he would. Instead Bougainville hastened on across the bridge over the river and then pulled up the bridge. Rogers halted his pursuit not thinking it wise to attempt a crossing when the French had a breastwork on the other side. He returned to St. Jean to meet Haviland who arrived that evening.

While Rogers was chasing the fleeing French on the 30th, Jenks and the rest of the army set out from their encampment in bateaux and other vessels about 10 a.m.. They passed by the battered French fort at Isle-aux-Noix and headed down river. Along the way some of the French were discovered along the shore, but they quickly took to their heels when the light infantry went ashore. The troops landed at St. Jean and were ordered to pitch their tents. As they were in enemy territory they kept their arms and ammunition close by.

The next morning the troops worked on building breastworks in the rain. Orders soon came to halt work and get ready to move, although it would not be until the following day, September 1, that the army struck their tents and set off downriver about 3 p.m.. Six miles downriver they arrived at St. Theresa where they found Canadian women and children, but no men. The army encamped for the night and then started entrenching the next day.

Rogers, meanwhile, had been near Chambly rounding up inhabitants and having them take the oath of allegiance to the King of England, which many of the people appeared happy to do so as to keep their possessions.

At St. Theresa part of the troops continued to toil away at the breastworks almost completing them. Some of the men went out and helped the Canadians get in their harvest, while about 1,000 troops and several cannons under the command of Darby set out to take Fort Chambly. Rogers and his rangers joined him there where the fort's garrison of 50 men surrendered without a fight.

Haviland soon sent Rogers off to make contact with Murray. Haviland would not be long in reaching Montreal. New France was almost done.

Chapter 11
New France Surrenders: September-December, 1760

B y September 6, Amherst's army had arrived at Lachine. While some of the provincials remained with the boats, the rest of the army quickly moved toward Montreal stopping for the night within sight of it. Some of his artillery was brought up during the night.

Inside Montreal the situation was grim. The three Anglo-Americans that were soon to be outside the city numbering around 17,000 men combined. Levis and Vaudreuil could muster only 2,500 regulars or so.[61] There simply were not enough men, guns and provisions to properly defend the city. There were no works to withstand a siege and the militia had gone home to see to their families and the Indians had made peace with the

---

[61] By the 7th Murray would arrive, followed by Haviland on the 8th.

British. There was nothing to do but surrender.

At daybreak on the 7th, Vaudreuil sent Bougainville with a message to Amherst to ask for a cessation of arms until it could be determined whether a peace had concluded in Europe. Amherst refused the request and replied bluntly that he had come to take Canada and "did not intend to take anything less."[62]If Vaudreuil had any terms of capitulation to propose he had until noon as the cease-fire would end then.

In the meantime the British continued to prepare for the siege of Montreal. Before the deadline, Vaudreuil sent a list of articles for the surrender of New France which included the surrender of troops not only in Montreal, but elsewhere such as Detroit and Michilimackinac. Vaudreuil

An East View of Montreal by Thomas Patten (Library and Archives Canada).

[62]Amherst, *Journal*, 246.

wanted the troops surrendered with honours of war and paroled to France. He was also concerned about the well being of the colonists who stayed in Canada, not only in regards to their property, but also their Catholic faith.

Amherst was very agreeable for the most part to the terms in regards to the civilians keeping their laws and customs as long as it was consistent to the allegiance to the British crown. Amherst also allowed for the free exercise of the Catholic faith. French law would remain as it was in regards to civil matters, but criminal matters would fall under martial law.

It was a different manner for the French troops. They had to lay down their arms and not serve in the present war. They would be sent to France without their colours. As far as Amherst was concerned the French troops had excited their Indians allies to commit barbarities during the war and there would be no surrender of honour for them.

Levis upon hearing this was livid and demanded that Vaudreuil end talks immediately. If Vaudreuil did not want to defend Montreal, he should allow the regulars to go to Ile Sainte-Helene where they would fight and die with honour. Vaudreuil said no. The terms were generous to the inhabitants and he would not ruin it for Levis and his officers' honour. He did give them time to burn their colours though. The following day, Monday September 8, 1760, Vaudreuil signed the article of capitulation.

With Canada in British hands the provincials with Haviland were sent back to Crown Point. The Connecticut provincials that had accompanied Amherst were sent on to Oswego and Fort Stanwix to finish the works there, while the New Jersey and New York provincials headed upriver to Fort William Augustus and repair the works there.

Major Rogers received written orders on September 12 from Amherst directing him to take two companies of rangers and head for Detroit to accept the surrender of the fort there from the French. By the end of November the British colours were flying over the post at Detroit.

In December, Rogers attempted to reach the French post at Michilimackinac, located between Lake Huron and Lake Michigan, but was turned back due to onset of winter. The surrender of this post would have to wait until spring. Another ranger party was more successful in accepting the surrender of French posts southwest of Detroit.

Although Canada was in British hands, the Seven Years War continued in both Europe and North America. Expeditions would be mounted by the British to capture Dominica, Martinique and Havana, Cuba. An expedition would also be conducted to recapture Newfoundland that was briefly captured by a French force that slipped past the Royal Navy. The Treaty of Paris signed in 1763 ended the world war between England and France. With the signing of the treaty Canada was officially surrendered to the British.

The last campaign that gave the death blow to New France was remarkable as Amherst himself would comment: "I believe never three Armys setting out from different & very distant Parts from each other, Joyned in the Center, as was intended, better than we did, and it could not fail of having the effect of which I have just now seen the consequence."[63] Canada was now part of the British Empire.

[63] *Ibid.*, 247.

Appendix A:
Post-war Careers of the Key 1760 Personalities

British and American

Amherst, Jeffery – As commander-in-chief of British forces in North America, he organized campaigns not only against the French in the West Indies, but also against Indian unrest on the North American frontier such as the Cherokee uprising from 1759-1761 and the "Pontiac uprising" in 1763. Late that year Amherst was recalled for his mishandling of this Indian crisis. During the American Revolution, Amherst was asked by the King to resume his role as commander of British forces in North America which he refused. Instead he was commander-in-chief in Britain. Amherst died in 1797.

Gage, Thomas – After Amherst was recalled in late 1763, Gage took over his position. He kept this post until 1775 when he was recalled at the beginning of the American

Revolution. He died in 1787.

Haviland, William – Haviland went on to serve in the capture of Martinique and Havana, Cuba in 1762. He served on Amherst's staff in England during the American Revolution and in 1779 was given command of the Western District. He died in 1784.

Johnson, Sir William – Johnson would go onto play a leading role in Indian affairs for the next fourteen years. At the same time his land holding would continue to grow considerably as did his wealth. He died while conducting an Indian conference in 1774.

Loring Joshua – After the war Loring saw some service on Lake Erie during the Pontiac Uprising. In 1767, he retired to his Roxbury estate and stayed there until the American Revolution broke out. Loring went to England where he died in 1781.

Murray, James – Murray became governor of the province of Quebec in 1764. He held the post for two years. During the American Revolution he made a valiant defense of Fort St. Philip, Minorca for about seven months against French and Spanish forces before being forced to surrender. He died in 1794.

Rogers, Robert – Rogers's finest hour was during the Seven Years' War. After the war he was appointed commandant of Fort Michilimackinac. There he sent out an expedition to find the legendary Northwest Passage. While commandant at this post, he was charged with treason and later acquitted, but not before his career was ruined. Plagued by debt, Rogers headed to England to try to alleviate his money problems. During the American Revolution he would command two Loyalist units. He died in 1795 in poverty.

French and Canadian

Bougainville, Louis-Antione de – In June of 1763, Bougainville was appointed a naval captain and in the coming years would make quite name for himself as an explorer. He would see action again against the British during the American Revolution. He died in 1811.

Bourlamaque, Francois-Charles de – Bourlamaque was made governor of Guadeloupe and died in 1764.

Levis, Francois Gaston – Levis returned to France in late November 1760. Released from his terms of capitulation in February of 1761, Levis served in Germany during the end of the Seven Years' War. In 1765, he became governor of Artois, a former province in Northern France. Interesting enough Levis kept up a correspondence with Murray during the siege of Fort St. Philip and even helped him get passage with his officers through France to England after the fall of the fort.

Pouchot, Pierre – Pouchot returned to France in 1761. He was killed in 1769 during the war in Corsica.

Vaudreuil de Cavagnial, Pierre de Rigaud,– The last governor of New France arrived in late November in France. Blamed in part for the loss of New France, Vaudrueil was sent to the Bastille on March 30, 1762. He was out by May and exonerated at his trial in December 1763. He died in France in 1778.

Appendix B:
'A Journal Kept by Colonel Nathaniel Woodhull'

Nathaniel Woodhull was born in Mastic, Long Island on December 30, 1722. During the French and Indian war he served at Ticonderoga and the expedition against Fort Frontenac in 1758 as a major. During the 1760 campaign, now promoted to Colonel, he commanded the 3rd Regiment of New York Provincials. After the war he married and settled down in Suffolk County and became a prosperous farmer. At the start of the American Revolution Woodhull was elected to the New York Provincial Congress. During the revolution he sided with the Patriots where he, as a brigadier-general in the militia, served at the battle of Long Island in 1776. He was wounded and captured there and would later die of his wounds that same year.

Albany, June 11th, 1760 – We struck our tents and marched to Schenectady, and encamped on the little island; the first regiment began their march from Schenectady for Oswego on the 12th; the second regiment for the fort at Oneida Lake on the 13th, and the third regiment on the 14th, for Fort Stanwix. We went about eight miles, when we encamped, and waited until ten o'clock, on the morning of the 15th, for the rear of the batteaux. We had prayers this morning, and then set out with the whole again. I had in my regiment 52 batteaux, and 800 barrels of provisions. We encamped about two miles below Fort William. On the 16th, we struck our tents, and went on.

We encamped on the 20th within two mile of the Little Falls, and waited there for the 1st and 2nd Regiments to get over the Falls. On the 23rd, we marched and encamped at the Falls; on the 25th we marched two miles above and encamped. On the 26th, we marched to Fort Karamay, where we drew provisions; on the 27th, we marched 12 miles; on the 28th, we went to (illegible); we got to Fort Stanwix on the 29th, and on the 3^d of July, we marched from that fort, and encamped at Fort Beal. On the 4th, we encamped at the neck, on the 5th at the west end of Oneida Lake; on the 6th, at the Three River Rift; on the 7th, at the falls, and on the 8th, we reached Oswego.

General Amherst arrived here the next day, and on the 15th, our vessels arrived here from Niagara.

August 8th. – The Grenadier Companies and Light Infantry Companies of each Regiment, and Capt'n Ogden's and Wait's Companies of Rangers, set out to take an advanced post under the command of Colonel (illegible);

the rest of the army left Oswego on the 10th, under the command of General Amherst, and encamped on a creek, about 30 miles from Oswego; the front got in about sunset; the rear did not get in until near midnight, many of the bateaux sticking fast on the beach all night, and several of them being stove and rendered unfit for service. After mending what we could of them, we set out again the next day, at 10 o'clock, and encamped at another creek, about 8 miles further; both very good harbors.

On the 12th, we set out again, and encamped in a fine bay. On the 13th, we set out at 9 o'clock, marching in three columns: the regulars on the right; the Connecticut and Jersey troops in the centre; and the Yorkers on the left, and encamped on Col. Robinson's bay; on the 14th, we set out at 10 o'clock, and encamped on Holdeman's island, where the regulars drew provisions. On the 15th, at 9 o'clock, we set out again, in three columns; the regulars on the right, the Jersey and Connecticut troops on the left, and the Yorkers in the centre. We entered the River St. Lawrence about 11 o'clock; we went about 20 miles down the river to our advance post, and there I encamped about five o'clock in the afternoon. Orders were immediately given for all Provincials to draw four days' provisions, and to examine all our arms and ammunition. On the 16th, at 10 o'clock, we set out again, and encamped at Point Berry, about 3 miles from Oswagorche, where we heard the cannon fire from the vessel. On the 17th, the Redows engaged her by daylight, and at 7 o'clock, they took her; there were 50 sailors and 60 marines on board of her; they had 3 men killed and 17 wounded, ten of whom died by the next day; we had only one man killed and one wounded; at 12 o'clock, we set out again, and encamped at Oswagorche, at 4 o'clock in the afternoon, with the whole army. There we found a good many Indians and squaws.

On the 18th, at 2 o'clock in the afternoon, all the regulars and rangers, and Lyman's and Naylor's Regiments, set out with the vessel taken from the French and the Redows, to attack the fort on the island; the fort and the vessels began to exchange shots. As the Batteaux and the Redows were passing the fort, a shot struck one of them, and a ball went thro' another, which killed two New Yorkers, and another struck a batteau, which broke a man's leg. They then took possession of the islands below the Fort, and began their batteries on the points of two of the islands, each about 600 yards of the fort. On the morning of the 19th, the vessel and fort began their fire at each other; the firing continued until about 10 o'clock, when it ceased on both sides. The Gunner was killed on the vessel. The three New York Regiments were ordered to march by the fort with all their artillery in the evening. On the morning of the 20th, we encamped; we continued at work on our batteries without firing, and the French only firing a few cannon, without doing any damage. There are several very good islands here, which are improved with buildings on them and plenty of corn, beans, squashes, and cabbages, with some hogs and fowls, but they were all deserted by the inhabitants as soon as we came in sight.

On the 21st, we still continued at work, making fascines and preparing our artillery and batteries, the French still very careful of their powder and ball. At ten o'clock, they began the fire briskly; they killed five men, three of them with one ball; at night they ceased firing until the next morning.

22nd. – In the morning they began to fire briskly from the fort again, and continue until 12 o'clock firing, and then ceased; they killed four of our men, and wounded several more. 23rd, at seven, in the morning, we opened our three batteries, and the batteries and vessels all began their fire at the fort together, the fort seldom returned the compliment; at 11 o'clock the vessels were ordered to fall down in a line near the fort, with men to fire from their round-tops, with small arms, which occasioned a heavy fire on both sides. The Onneadaga ran aground, upon which her brave Commodore Lowrin struck his colors, and called for quarter, and sent an officer into the fort, notwithstanding he was so near one of our Batteries; but the English colors were soon again hoisted on board, we continued the whole day firing shell and shot at the fort, and all night.

24th.- We still continue firing.

25th.- At four o'clock in the afternoon, the French beat a parley, and at 6 o'clock, the Garrison surrendered themselves prisoners of war, when the Grenadiers immediately marched in and took possession of the Fort. Mons. Pasheau was commandant of the Fort, with 350 men; sixty of whom were killed, and twenty wounded.

26th.- We spent in loading our cannon in the Batteaux again and making all the preparation necessary to proceed.

27th.- We sent the prisoners to Oswego, and Capt. Prescot set out for England, with an express from Gen'l Amherst.

28th.- Still preparing our boats and clearing the Islands, Amherst and Deal.

29th.- As yesterday.

30th.- We received orders to send all our sick to Oswagorche, and the whole army to be ready to march the next day; at night, orders were given for the second Brigade of Regulars, the light infantry Grenadier companies, Schuyler's, Lyman's and Fitch's Regiments, with part of the artillery, to strike their tents at seven o'clock the next morning, and the rest to be ready to march the next day.

31st. – They marched at 11 o'clock.

September 1st. – The rest of the army set out at 10 o'clock, and encamped at Cat's Island, about twenty-five miles from Fort William Augustus.

2nd.- We set out at six o'clock, and got into Lake St. Francis about four o'clock in the afternoon, and encamped on an island about miles in the lake.

Sept. 3rd.- We laid still the whole day by reason of wet weather.

4th.- We set out at 6 o'clock, in the morning, with orders not to plunder any thing from the inhabitants, on pain of death; we got over the Lake St. Francis about 9 o'clock; after we had proceeded about three miles, we came to a bad rift, where several batteaux and about twenty men were lost.

We got to the Cedars about twelve o'clock, where we halted; here there are settlements for about 4 miles on the river. We set out again about 2 o'clock, and found bad rifts for 4 miles; here we lost a good many Batteaux and men; the front of the army went about six miles and encamped on Isle Paroot, but four regiments did not get over the falls and part of the artillery. 5th, we passed over with all our Batteaux, and encamped with our whole army on Isle Paroot, where there is a very good settlement.

The General gave orders for all the French on the islands to take the oath of allegiance, and they should enjoy their estates. A considerable number came to the General this day, and the owner of the Island, and took the oath. Two expresses came to the General this day; one from Gen'l Murray, and the other from Col. Haviland, with news of St. John's and the Isle au Nois being taken, and Montreal invested.

6th.- We marched at 6 o'clock, with the whole army thro' a fine settled country, about 20 miles, and landed at the King's store-house, about 2 miles above the falls; the army immediately landed all their men, excepting two on each boat, excepting the New Yorkers, Fitches and Woster's regiments, and marched for Montreal. The Yorkers immediately furnished a party to draw the light artillery down, and 300 were drafted to draw down the 24-pounders, the same evening. Fitches' and Woster's

Regiments were to remain until further orders.

We have passed by four famous churches; one of which is at Cockawago, where the Indian town is. We are now on the island of Montreal, which begins near the island of Paroot, and from the Store House to Montreal, is nine miles; the island is about 26 miles long; the name of this place is Lachine. The army got before the walls of Montreal this evening, and lay on their arms all night.

7th.- A flag of truce was sent to General Amherst from Mons. Vaudreiule, for a cessation of arms, until he could hear from France, to know whether there was not a peace concluded. The General allowed the cessation until 12 o'clock.

There were orders sent the Batteaux of all the Regiments but the 3rd New York Regiments and Woster's, to be immediately brought down to the camp.

The cessation was afterwards continued until the morning of the 8th, when the articles of capitulation were signed; which provided that all soldiers were to be transported to France, and not to take up arms during the continuance of the war, and the inhabitants to enjoy every thing that belonged to them, and to be governed by the Laws of England.

9th.- We marched and encamped with the whole army.

10th.- We received orders to march up the River St. Lawrence. Laprairie lies over against Montreal.

11th.- The Connecticut regiments set out for Oswego.
12th, the Jersey and three New York Regiments began their

march from Montreal for Fort Augustus, and encamped at Lachine, and continued there the 13th and 14th, until 3 o'clock in the afternoon, when we set out again at Point Claire, where there is a large church, and a very pleasant place, where we bought plenty of sheep and fowls.

15th.- The wind blowing hard, we were obliged to continue here this day. 16th, we set out early, and encamped a mile below the church, at Point Cedar; 17th, we went about five miles, and encamped above the falls; 18th, we set out at nine o'clock, in the morning, and encamped within a mile of the Lake St. Francis; 19th, we encamped on an island, about six miles from the west end of the Lake; 20th, we encamped below the three mile rift; 21st, we encamped about 15 miles from Fort Augustus; 22nd, we encamped about seven miles from the Fort.

23d.- We got to Devil's island at 2 o'clock, and encamped on it.

25th.- Began to work at the Fort, and continued to work at the Fort until October 19th, when we received orders to be ready to march the next day, at 12 o'clock; 20th, we left Fort Wm. Augustus at five o'clock in the afternoon, and went about 20 miles, and at ten o'clock, at night, we put up; 21st, we set out again, at 9 o'clock, and went another fifteen miles of the Lake, where I encamped about sunset, when it began to snow, and continued snowing until 8 o'clock, on the 22nd, and then cleared. We put off immediately, and encamped on an island about 40 miles from Oswego, at eleven o'clock, at night; the wind sprang up from the southeast, when I was obliged to put off for the main land, which was distant about three miles. The wind blowing very hard, we were obliged to haul up our Batteaux.

23rd.- The wind still blowing very hard, we were obliged to continue here, as also the four following days. The wind blew continually from the Southwest, West, and Northwest, with squalls of snow, hail, and rain, in such a manner as I never saw before.

27th.- Our provisions growing scarce, a number this day started for Oswego, by land.

Bibliography

Published Primary Sources:

Amherst, Jeffery. *The Journal of Jeffery Amherst.* J. Clarence Webster (editor).Toronto: The Ryerson Press, 1933

Anonymous. *An Impartial Account of Lieut. Colonel Bradstreet's Expedition to Fort Frontenac.* London: T. Wilcox, 1759.

Bonin, Charles "Joliceur", *Memoir of a French and Indian War Soldier.* Andrew Gallup (editor). Westminster, Maryland: Heritage Books, Inc, 1993.

Hawks, John. *Orderly Book and Journal of Major John Hawks on the Ticonderoga-Crown Point Campaign, under General Jeffery Amherst 1759-1760.* Published by the

Society of Colonial Wars in the State of New York, through the Historian and Committee of Historical Documents. New York: H.K Brewer & Co., 1911.

Hervey, William. *Journals of the Hon. William Hervey in North America and Europe From 1755-1814; with Order Books at Montreal, 1760-1763. With Memoirs and Notes.* St. Edmund's: Paul & Mathew, Butter Market, 1906.

Holden, David. *Journal Kept by David Holden of Groton, Mass. During the Latter Part of the French and Indian War February 20-November 29, 1760.* Cambridge: John Wilson and Son, 1889.

Jenks, Samuel. *Diary of Captain Samuel Jenks during the French and Indian War 1760.* Cambridge: John Wilson and Son, 1890, reprinted from Proceedings of the Massachusetts Historical Society, 1890.

Johnstone, Chevalier. *The Campaign of 1760 in Canada.* Quebec: Literary and Historical Society of Quebec, 1887.

Kirk, Robert. *Through So Many Dangers: The Memoirs and Adventures of Robert Kirk, Late of the Royal Highland Regiment.* Ian McCulloch and Timothy Todish (editors). Fleischmanns, New York: Purple Mountain Press, 2004.

Knox, John. *An Historical Journal of the Campaigns in North America Vol. II.* Toronto: The Champlain Society,

1914.

Murray, General James. *Manuscript relating to the Early History of Canada; Journal of the Siege of Quebec, 1760.* Quebec: Middleton & Dawson, 1871.

Pouchot, M. *Memoir Upon the Late War in North America between France and England 1755-1760 Vol. 1.* Franklin B. Hough (editor and translator). Roxbury, Mass.: W. Elliot Woodward, 1866.

Robert, Rogers. *The Annotated and Illustrated Journals of Major Robert Rogers.* Annotated by Timothy J. Todish. Fleischmanns, New York: Purple Mountain Press, 2002

Sullivan, James (editor). *The Papers of Sir William Johnson 14 Vols.* Albany: University of New York, 1921-1965.

Woodhull, Nathaniel. 'A Journal Kept by General Nathaniel Woodhull', *Historical Magazine* September 1861, Vol. V. No. 9.

Secondary Sources:

Allen, Robert S. *His Majesty's Indian Allies: The British Indian Policy in the Defence of Canada, 1774-1815.* Toronto: Dundurn Press, 1992.

Anderson, Fred. *Crucible of War: The Seven Years' War and the Fate of Empire in British North America, 1754-1766.* New York: Vintage Books, 2001.

Beer, George Louis. *British Colonial Policy, 1754-1765.* New York: The Macmillian Company, 1922

Brumwell, Stephen. *Paths of Glory: The Life and Death of General James Wolfe.* Montreal & Kingston: McGill and Queen's University Press, 2006.

Brumwell, Stephen. *Redcoats: The British Soldier and War in the Americas, 1755-1763.*New York: Cambridge University Press, 2002.

Brumwell, Stephen. *White Devil: A True Story of War, Savagery, and Vengeance in Colonial America.* De Capo Press, 2004.

Campbell, Alexander V. *The Royal American Regiment: An Atlantic Microcosm, 1755-1772.* Norman: University of Oklahoma Press, 2010.

Chartrand, Rene. *The Forts of New France in Northeast America 1600-1763.* Oxford: Osprey Publishing, 2008.

Cuneo, John R. *Robert Rogers of the Rangers.* Ticonderoga, New York: Fort Ticonderoga Museum, 1988 (originally published by New York: Oxford University Press, 1959).

Downes, Randolph C. *Council Fires on the Upper Ohio.* Pittsburgh: University of Pittsburgh Press, 1940.

Dunnigan, Brian Leigh. *Siege – 1759: The Campaign Against Niagara.* Youngstown, New York: Old Fort Niagara Association, 1996.

Flexner, James Thomas. *Lord of the Mohawks: A Biography of Sir William Johnson.* Boston: Little, Brown and Company, 1959.

Forbes, Archibald L.L.D. *The "Black Watch"; The Record of an Historic Regiment.* New York: Charles Scribner's Sons, 1897.

Hough, Franklin. *A History of St. Lawrence and Franklin Counties, New York.* Albany: Little & Co., 1853.

Jennings. Francis. *Empire of Fortune: Crowns, Colonies & Tribes in the Seven Years War in America.* New York: W.W. Norton & Company, 1988.

Johnson, Michael G. *American Woodland Indians.* London: Osprey Publishing Ltd., 1990.

Kingsford, William. *The History of Canada.* Toronto: Roswell & Hutchison, 1893.

Long, J.C. *Lord Jeffery Amherst: A Soldier of the King.* New

York: The MacMillan Company, 1933.

Loescher, Burt Garfield. *Gensis: Roger's Rangers, The First Green Berets.* Westminster, Maryland: Heritage Books Inc, 2000 (originally published in 1969).

MacLeod, Peter D. *The Canadian Iroquois and the Seven Years' War.* Toronto: Dundurn Press, 1996.

Mahon, Major-General R. H. *Life of General the Hon. James Murray, A Builder of Canada.* London, 1921.

Mante, Thomas. *The History of the Late War in North America.* London, 1772.

May, Robin. *Wolfe's Army.* London: Osprey Publishing Ltd., 1974.

McConnell, Michael N. *Army & Empire: British Soldiers on the American Frontier, 1758-1775.* Lincoln: University of Nebraska Press, 2004.

McIlwraith, Jean N. *The Makers of Canada: Sir Frederic Haldimand.* Toronto: Morang & Co., Limited, 1905.

Parkman, Francis. *Montcalm and Wolfe.* New York: Collier Books, 1962

O'Toole, Finan. *White Savage: William Johnson and the*

Invention of America, Albany: State University of New York Press, 2005.

Rogers, Robert J. *Rising Above Circumstances: The Rogers Family in Colonial America*. Beford, Quebec: Sheltus & Picard Inc., 1998.

Stacey, C.P. "Jeffery Amherst", *Dictionary of Canadian Biography Vol. IV,* Toronto: University of Toronto Press, 1979. Also found at Dictionary of Canadian Biographies Online. http://www.biographi.ca.

Stacey, C.P. *Quebec, 1759: The Siege and the Battle*. Toronto: The MacMillan Company of Canada Limited, 1959.

Stanley, George F. *New France: The Last Phase 1744-1760*. Toronto: McClelland and Stewart, 1968.

Steele, I.K. *Guerillas and Grenadiers*. Toronto: The Ryerson Press, 1969.

Stoetzel, Donald I. *Encyclopedia of the French and Indian War in North America 1754-1763*. Westminister, Maryland: Heritage Books Inc., 2008.

Stone, William L. *The Life and Times of Sir William Johnson, Bart. Vol. II*. Albany: J. Munsell, 1865.

Todish, Timothy J. *America's First First World War; The*

French and Indian War, 1754-1763. Ogden, Utah: Eagle's View Publishing Company, 1988.

Vaugeois, Denis. *The Last French and Indian War*. Montreal: McGill-Queen's University, 2002.

Index

Shirley, William – 41.
Solomon, Captain – 42, 110,
Sorel – 73, 74, 75, 76, 77.
Ticonderoga - 3, 8, 17, 22, 56,
125.
Thorton, Joshua – 96, 97, 100.
Trois-Rivieres – 69, 70, 71, 72,
76.
Tute, Captain - 16n.
Varenne – 78, 79.
Vaudreuil de Cavagnial, Pierre
de Riguad– 24, 25, 111, 112,
116, 117, 118, 124, 132.

Vauquelin, Jean – 39.
Waite, Joseph – 59, 126.
Warren, Peter - 6.
Wigwam Martinique – 42, 47.
Williamson, Adam – 90, 97.
Williamson, George – 81, 89,
92, 94.
Willyamos, Samuel – 60.
Wolfe, James - 7, 8, 12, 14, 15,
17, 19, 34.
Woodhull, Nathaniel – 58, 93,
125.
Young, Henry - 10, 11.

ABOUT THE AUTHOR

Michael Phifer, who lives with his wife Robin and two dogs in rural Eastern Ontario, has written numerous articles on military and frontier history for such magazines as Military Heritage, Muzzle Blasts and other publications. He has also authored a number of books dealing with the American Revolution, the War of 1812 and the Old West. He is an avid blackpowder shooter and works as an historical interpreter.

19559819R00086

Made in the USA
Charleston, SC
31 May 2013